we
are
each
other

we are each other

Jess Mills

LEAP

First published in the UK in 2026 by LEAP
An imprint of Bonnier Books UK
5th Floor, HYLO, 105 Bunhill Row,
London, EC1Y 8LZ

Copyright © Jess Mills, 2026

All rights reserved.

No part of this publication may be reproduced, stored or transmitted in any form or by any means, electronic, mechanical, photocopying or otherwise, without the prior written permission of the publisher.

The right of Jess Mills to be identified as Author of this work has been asserted by her in accordance with the Copyright, Designs and Patents Act, 1988.

A CIP catalogue record for this book is available from the British Library.

Hardback ISBN: 9781785124709

Also available as an ebook and an audiobook

1 3 5 7 9 10 8 6 4 2

Design and Typeset by Envy Design Ltd
Printed and bound by CPI (UK) Ltd, Croydon CR0 4YY

Every reasonable effort has been made to trace copyright holders of material reproduced in this book, but if any have been inadvertently overlooked the publishers would be glad to hear from them.

The authorised representative in the EEA is
Bonnier Books UK (Ireland) Limited.
Registered office address: Block B, The Crescent Building
Northwood, Santry
Dublin 9, D09 C6X8, Ireland
compliance@bonnierbooks.ie

www.bonnierbooks.co.uk

For you, Mum.

— *Contents* —

Preface 1

— *Spring 2017* — 3

— *Summer 2017* — 53

— *Autumn 2017* — 91

— *Winter 2017* — 115

— *Spring 2018* — 133

— *Summer 2018* — 201

— *Autumn 2018* — 213

— *Epilogue* — 225

— *Acknowledgements* — 231

— *Preface* —

My mother's name was Tessa Jowell. She was elected Labour member of Parliament for Dulwich and West Norwood in 1992, a constituency in south- east London she served devotedly for 23 years.

Over her 50 years of public service, she became known as 'the people's politician', a rare accolade in British politics that signalled her unique and outstanding brand of authenticity, her decency and her ability to see and advocate for the humanity of the people she was elected to serve.

She had some standout professional achievements of which she was hugely proud, including her part in delivering the 2012 Olympics in London and leading some of Labour's most transformational public health initiatives. She was awarded many honorary titles in recognition of her profound contribution to tackling inequality in British society. She was a dame, Baroness of Brixton, a privy councillor, a secretary of state, a member of Parliament – but to everyone who knew her, she was just 'Tess'.

To me, she was 'Mum'. If she was ever asked what her proudest achievement was, she would always, without hesitation, say, 'My family, of course.'

Shortly after I became a mother for the first time in 2017, Mum suffered a sudden loss of consciousness and within days was diagnosed with brain cancer, from which she died a little less than a year later. Her extraordinary life was celebrated and her untimely death mourned across the spectrum of British Society, but nowhere more so than in the epicentre of our life together.

What follows in these pages is not an account of the public person she was. This is the story of us: mother, daughter and granddaughter, walking on both sides of life and death together in that defining year.

— *Spring 2017* —

'Jess, can you hear me? Paramedics are on their way, but I won't make it to you in time now... When the next contraction comes, please, listen to my instructions.'

But I am beyond reach of the midwife's voice, which is bellowing from my phone in fractured echoes. As the next contraction detonates in the middle earth of my body, my spine contorts like a whip, releasing a roar from the base of my throat which sounds like the truth of an animal in pain. Glistening crimson waters suddenly release onto the inside of my thighs. Then, like the sky between storms, stillness returns. Birth is as close as my breath – dangerously so, because my boyfriend Finn and I are alone. All I can hear is the pounding noise of my heart in my ears until the midwife's voice reappears like the coastguard to a ship lost at sea.

'Finn, can you hear me? I need to know if you have ever delivered a baby before.'

'No. No, I haven't,' he replies, his voice compressed by a choke of panic. Both of us are crouched down on our knees, my left arm grips tighter around his neck.

Then, as all the muscles of courage are cradling me, I reach my right hand down between my legs and touch something, just inside me, which, to my disbelief, I realise is not my body. I can't steady my hand, which is trembling at this sensation: my fingertips, touching the hair on the crown of my baby's head for the first time. In the street below the bathroom window, the paramedics are arriving in an eruption of sirens and refracting blue light that dances across the room's newly painted walls. Within moments, the thundering sounds of fists at our front door become the rustling sound of two paramedics clambering into the bathroom and over my naked arching spine.

As they do, I can hear the motion of another body climbing the stairs, a body whose movements and weight I know completely. Her voice is now at the door of our tiny bathroom and it reaches out to me like an outstretched arm over the paramedics assembling gas and air tanks and clean towels between us.

'I'm here, sweetheart. Jessie, darling, I'm here. I'm here.' It's Mum. At once, I know I am safe. I can let it happen now. Mum has made it, just in time.

Because here it is: the moment I have been trying to imagine and prepare for, for the past nine months and the whole of my adult life. Yet how could I have imagined the unimaginable?

As the next contraction ignites in my core, I feel myself split from human to mammal in that place that connects me to every living thing. I am thrust with a force both within and beyond me to roar with surrender and I push: the crown of its head, the width of its shoulders, the span of its ribcage and then an eruption of limbs beyond my skin, through a furnace of white-hot agony between my legs. As this happens, I feel the thin veil between new life and death collapse. I am both inside and outside of time.

For a moment, I am not sure if I am still here.

Until I hear the words, 'It's a little girl, and she's

perfect!' announced by one of the paramedics at my tail end blocking the bathroom door.

Mum's arms stretch out to me over their back. Her bright blue eyes are sparkling with relief and the very particular look of her love that she directs right into me. The four people arranged like an installation around me all collapse into tears of relief and cheer. The ordinary cataclysm and mystery of childbirth is filling the space between us all. The walls feel weak. My arms buckle like the legs of a newborn deer and I slump at their feet, bloodied, shaking, weeping with relief and shock in equal measure. I cannot believe it. A daughter: my daughter.

I'm moved to my bed across the landing with her in my arms. Her skin is reddening; her eyes are blinking slowly, luminous black and serene. An onset of crystal-clear euphoria ascends my spine. My eyes regain focus, comprehending the animated reality of her body that now exists beyond me. I have been divided. With the weirdness of our birth-drenched house around us, I know that motherhood has already changed me. My daughter's life has begun.

◆ ◆ ◆

We Are Each Other

Finn and I decide to call our daughter Ottilene, though she instantly becomes known as 'Ottie'. The air around Ottie forms new weather. I cannot comprehend her. I cannot comprehend myself. I feel like I have been redrawn, now with new edges that extend beyond the page of my body.

Ottie is a soft, heavenly storm of spiralling dark, downy hair and pink, pillowy lips. She has Finn's wide-set black eyes, glistening pools that look so deep you could fall into them. The skeletal mechanism of her body retracts into the foetal position when she rests; she hasn't unfolded from being in my womb yet.

Every new day that passes feels like a landmark. The only way I can measure time is by Ottie's age in the number of days: she is one day, two days, one week, ten days old. In the haze of newborn motherhood, twilight feels constant and the nights so long, tender and raw that every morning, as the thin beginnings of morning light start to glow behind the curtains, I feel simultaneously broken and triumphant that we made it through to the next day. Finn has been sleeping in the spare bedroom so he is rested enough to be able to look after us in the day, but it means I haven't slept for longer than an hour at a time since she was born. The last few mornings when I've taken Ottie through to him, I've kissed her tiny nose and feather-soft cheeks and laid her onto his chest with eyes full of giant tears from exhaustion and a sharp tug at my solar plexus that makes my heart pound hard and fast whenever we are separated.

My brain is still working hard to assimilate the moments that confirm Ottie is real and that I really am a mother now. Moments like seeing mine and Finn's discarded clothes on the wooden floorboards next to the bed, which now include breast pads and her soft pink, green or white baby grows. Or the sensation of her warm and hungry mouth at my breast, which makes me gasp as it sends both a pain as sharp as glass through my breast and a feeling of simultaneous euphoria and overwhelm into my throat.

I am being sustained, mostly, by a potent and primal experience of this new maternal love which feels as mind altering as a drug. It makes my face look different. I caught myself in the mirror by our bed this morning and my pupils were so dilated, they made my eyes look deep set and entirely black. I looked feral.

We Are Each Other

It's making me behave differently too. My world has become the size of our bed and I guard over Ottie with eyes that are wild like a cat's.

However, most afternoons since she was born, Ottie and I have managed to hold court in bed while best friends and family have come to deliver combinations of presents, cakes and flowers. I haven't left the house in ten days. Mum has been with us each one, leaving only occasionally to go to the shops, from whence she returns with bags that rustle like a cluster of balloons, full of treats. The experience of sharing Ottie, new motherhood and new grandmotherhood with my mum has established itself with an immediate symbiosis. In this new intergenerational dynamic between the three of us, I am experiencing some of the purest feelings of contentment and gratitude I have ever felt in my life.

My mum has a way of making people feel like they are special in a way that is character defining. She has dedicated her entire life to public service, which I think is rooted in her rare ability to 'see' people in their humanity, one by one. But I have never seen her speak about anyone in the way she does about Ottie. I hear her on the phone downstairs talking to various friends with such exaltation and marvel in her voice that if you didn't know, you could be mistaken for thinking she was the only person who had ever witnessed the miracle and creation of life. On the phone to her friend Julia this morning: 'Oh, darling, you just cannot believe this baby, you just have to see her to believe her . . . No, no, but she is, she is *so* beautiful. Yes! I'm sure she smiled at me just now, she's very advanced, of course!' Hoots of laughter. 'Did you get the photos I sent yesterday? I've got loads more to send you. Oh my god, she's just unbelievable. You have to come and see her for yourself. I've already told Jessie we'll have Granny Thursdays when she's a bit bigger up at mine so I can have her the whole day then, so you can come and see her at mine too.'

I chuckle to myself, imagining the naturally less interested expressions of her many close friends who have been on the other end of the phone getting the same run down, humouring and indulging her. But it's very hard not to do that with Mum – her enthusiasm and warmth are so authentic, so irresistible, it disarms even the hardest of cynics.

We Are Each Other

Moment to moment, nothing has ever felt as *huge*, and made me feel as *small*, as new motherhood, and Mum has a way of making it all feel seen and important. She is the intimate witness of us in all our minutiae.

'So how many feeds did she have last night, then?'

'Ooh, she's holding my eye contact just a little bit more today, darling.' 'And what time did you wake up after taking her into Finn?'

'How are your boobs feeling?'

'I noticed you need more breast pads, darling.' Or just: 'How are you today, sweetheart?'

This is the question that means most because mostly people just ask how Ottie is. Mum can do this for me in a way that Finn can't because while he hasn't physically been through the cataclysm of birth, he has been at the coal face of her delivery and new parenthood with me. Mum has just enough distance and emotional separation, like she's in a 'watchtower' where she can see us, and what we need before we know it ourselves.

The last few evenings, Dad has turned up at our front door with a big Tupperware of dinner for us already made, which Finn, Mum, Dad and I have then congregated to eat, perched on our bed surrounded by discarded boxes of cupcakes, wet wipes and tiny pairs of socks from the afternoon spent in our newborn nest. Dad's cooking is a pillar of our family life. Against the backdrop of this vast and unfamiliar landscape of new motherhood, something as simple as the familiar taste of Dad's spaghetti Bolognese feels comforting. I suppose since I left home in my early twenties, in its most reductive form, this is what my family has been. It is the world I have returned to that remains unchanged, even when everything else may have changed beyond recognition. New motherhood has given me a new perspective and a deep sense of appreciation for this most basic function and purpose of family.

In the most practical sense, since having Ottie, we have needed our family to feed us, to share in the celebration of her and provide reassurance and confidence. And not just for me. Finn has been shellshocked since Ottie's birth too. When I was pregnant, I developed gestational diabetes, which makes childbirth very high risk. I was told it wasn't safe for me to have my baby in the birth centre with the midwife-led team because babies with diabetic mothers can present in very complicated ways at birth.

We Are Each Other

I would need to be under the care of an experienced obstetrician, with constant monitoring of me and the baby, right next to an operating theatre, due to the high chance of needing an emergency caesarean section.

Finn is a quietly spoken, stoic person. He is completely unneurotic and doesn't do melodrama. In the six years we've been together, I have never seen him look scared. But when the midwife told us down the phone that she wouldn't get to us in time, she knew, Finn knew and I knew that me and our unborn baby might be on the precipice of something catastrophic. From that moment until she was born, an expression of abject fear pulled all the colour from Finn's face, eyes and lips. Looking at him now as he's holding Ottie curled over his shoulder with one arm, eating a plate of spaghetti with the other, I can see a very faint suggestion of a blue line around his mouth still. The memory of her birth is still pulsating hot and sharp in my brain too, like shrapnel.

◆ ◆ ◆

Why doesn't anyone tell us? Women are told our whole lives that birth will be one of the most profound biological experiences we will have, but there is no mention at *all*, from *anyone*, that it is merely the opening scene to one of the most profound psychological events and that we should prepare for how we will be changed at a soul level after it too.

Everywhere around me on cards of congratulations I am seeing birth represented in pastel shades of pinks, yellows and blues. In images of bunnies and bears, of softness, cuteness and order. But all I know is: I have never felt as close to death as I did in birth. Death was there not simply as a thought, but as if the possibility of it was moving through me. Yet just as quickly as it was there, it was gone – replaced by the life-defining moment when my perfectly healthy baby was placed in my arms for the first time. In that instant, the utterly surreal, inexplicable awe and mystery of creation took centre stage instead. But those parts of birth, the life-altering experience of chaos and pain, near death and separation, have left their shadowy marks as evidence on my soul. The memories of it are still pulsating in the colours of burgundy and black: bludgeoned.

I feel so raw and skinless that I don't feel robust enough to hold the extreme paradox of it all. Maybe other women just don't feel like this, because if they did, then surely I would have known about it?

Then there's the physical stuff. My body feels like it's been hit by a train.

This morning, I walked around my bed to the bathroom and stood in the exact place where I gave birth, with Ottie curled into my neck. I stood in front of the mirror and looked at my full reflection with my feral eyes for the first time: it was completely unrecognisable to me. Huge, heavy, veiny breasts; bulging doughy stomach with a thin, dark line still tracing down the middle. I felt disembodied, as though I was inhabiting someone else. I quickly put my dressing gown on to cover myself up, which felt like wrapping a huge bandage around me. Then there are my internal wounds from birth that are still so deep and raw that I can't bear for Finn to tend to them – my mum is the only person who can see these parts of me without causing sharp pains and indignity to rise through my stomach.

I am 35 years old and have lived a fiercely independent life since my late teens. It is completely unforeseen that in becoming a mother, I would feel this intense need to be mothered myself. But the truth is that in becoming a mother, I feel mostly like a child.

Now I'm back in bed, Mum has come up with a cup of tea and one of her new purchases: a hot water bottle with a fluffy white cover on it to put on my lower back. She takes Ottie from me and I watch them with my eyes pinned to their every movement. Mum is as natural and at ease with my baby in her arms as if Ottie were one of her own limbs: folding up clean muslins with one hand, changing her nappy and buttoning her into her fresh baby grows with nimble, strong fingers. Patting her with just enough vigour, in that sweet spot in the middle of her back, so she lets out a belly-sized burp just after she's fed. I watch them hoping that that feeling of ease and confidence will soon be mine too.

Because in recent days, the fizz of newborn motherhood has started to flatten under cumulative, eye-splitting exhaustion. There are short pockets of time throughout the day and night when Ottie returns to her burrow of sleep and I lie next to her, staring at her with my wild eyes. My heart feels porous, with elemental love roaring through it, completely unprotected. So much so, that a few times in the last few days, I have felt the claws of vulnerability grip my stomach in a way that is so unsettling, it makes this new experience of maternal love feel like fear. It feels unsafe, completely terrifying, to be so entwined, to love someone this much. Within this slow shock and pain of our separation since birth, a rising fog of strange and unfamiliar anxiety has started to set in – one that makes me yearn for Ottie even when she is sleeping in my arms. I have had an unnerving awareness that those deep, dark shadows, the burgundy and black ones that have been in my peripheral vision since I gave birth, are starting to close in on me in an intrusive and menacing way. I am longing to go home into the epicentre of my family, to be in the place where everything is most safe and most familiar: Lower Farm.

◆ ◆ ◆

Lower Farm sits at the foot of the last Cotswold hill – an ancient, muscular, bucolic fortress that holds our tiny village in the most protected crook of its arm; a twinkling constellation in the dark, quiet night surrounding us. This is the pocket of the English countryside where my family has congregated throughout my life for weekends, Christmases, Easters and often for many weeks throughout the summer with my siblings and my six nieces.

There are five children in our family: my elder siblings Eleanor, Luke and Annie, born to my dad's first marriage, and me and my younger brother Matthew, my mum's only biological two, though the technical terminology of 'half' brothers and sisters has always felt like an insensitive distinction to a family that feels whole. Eleanor is 11 years older than me, Luke nine and Annie six. Matthew is two years younger. As the eldest of my mum's biological children, and the fourth-born of my dad's, I am both the eldest and second youngest in our line of siblings. Some of my earliest memories are of the cacophony of the five of us, then aged between one and 13, receiving Dad's scrambled eggs round our kitchen table at breakfast time or being in the bath with bubbles as high as our ears as Matthew and I lathered Annie's chocolate brown and Eleanor's blonde curls in lurid green children's shampoo.

When we were growing up, Annie, Luke and

We Are Each Other

Eleanor lived most of the time with their mum, 20 minutes from our house in north London, but would come over every other Thursday for the weekend. I remember vividly the feeling of the coarse, chestnut brown bristles of the mat by the front door under the skin of my legs as me and Matthew waited with our backs resting against the front door in anticipation of their arrival. It always felt like we had to wait forever for them to appear, but, once they did, we would run laps around the house like overexcited puppies chasing our tails, and the volume of the house would instantly crank up tenfold with the sound of Luke's booming baritone voice, Eleanor's belly laughs, and Annie and Mum getting straight into all their news.

From the moment they arrived, I wanted to be as physically close to them as possible. Luke was six foot two, even as a teenager, with bright green eyes and sandy brown hair. I remember the feeling of clambering up onto the height of his knees at the kitchen table, or cuddling up in between Eleanor and Annie on the sofa, wanting to be inside their teenage world with them. The sight of their weekend bags in the hallway, their leather or faded blue Levi's jean jackets hung over the banister exuding the faded smell of perfume, aftershave and cigarettes, their stories of new girlfriends, boyfriends, parties – by the time I was nine, I was totally enraptured by their adolescent energy.

I also remember vividly, at the end of every other weekend, after I heard the front door clunk shut behind them as they left to go back to their mum's, how disconcertingly empty and quiet the house suddenly was. I recall the impulse to immediately rummage through Annie's clothes to find one of her T-shirts that hung as long as a dress around my child-sized frame, of pulling the neckline up around my nose because it smelt like her. Yet, at the epicentre of this expansive family, where I felt our arms were always spread wide to each other, is the experience of a nuclear family: Matthew, Mum and Dad – who were the pillars of my day-to-day world, growing up.

Matthew and I are so different in lots of ways: when we were little, he had bright blond hair, while mine was dark brown; he's now a businessman and I'm a musician. When we were teenagers, he loved sports and being at home, while I was always with my friends and out the door at the mere sniff of a party. But I think we feel the experience of being alive in a very similar way. We have that very particular closeness and knowing between us that you can only really have with someone who you have been parented your entire life alongside. We are the same on our insides, both raised within the stability of our parents' love, which, as children, felt like a fortress. I can remember how it made us feel secure in the world. This, of course, is one of life's greatest privileges, and one that Matthew and I are lucky enough to share. Even though he's younger than me, as grown-ups now, he behaves towards me more like a big brother: he has inherited Mum's capacity to love, her emotional intelligence and sense of purpose, and all of Dad's generosity and joie de vivre.

When my siblings are at Lower Farm en masse now – which includes each of my elder siblings' children, my glorious six nieces – the house is full to bursting with us doing nothing. In the very rare moments when the noise drops, you can hear the woody 'tick-tock' of the old grandfather clock, each second delivered like a promise.

In a family where the demands of each of our lives, especially Mum's, could often feel relentless, Lower Farm is, above all, a refuge. Dad will often say that driving round the final bend of the lane that leads to our house, then closing the heavy wooden door to the clunk of the old letter box, is 'the moment you know the buggers can't get you'. Being at Lower Farm slows the pulse to a daily schedule of long pampering baths, idle walks down the lane and Dad's cycle of delicious meals with accompanying stages of puddings and booze.

Dad was born in 1944. His father was in MI5 and Dad's childhood was spent between England, Gibraltar and Jamaica, so that his father could follow the scent of his next assignment. His mother, my granny, was an anchor of love and stability for him, his brother and sister, but they were each sent off to boarding school in the depths of the Scottish Highlands for months at a time when they turned nine. Maybe this brutal severance from home when he was so young explains why he is such a homebody.

A retired lawyer, Dad is known for his largesse and hospitality. He is referred to as Mr Toad by his close

We Are Each Other

friends, in reference to the ostentatious character from Kenneth Grahame's book *The Wind in the Willows*. Like Mr Toad, Dad has an infectious joie de vivre. He is an old school bon viveur who wears jewel-coloured trousers and brightly coloured chequered shirts. A mischievous provocateur around the dinner table, he is always the advocate of another bottle of wine, with rounds of stiff whiskies to follow. He's the proud teller of filthy jokes, accompanied by bellyfuls of his own laughter and occasionally Mum's mortification, amid the thick smoke of his cigars and steam from rounds of espresso: this potent combination of smells is one of the most evocative of my childhood.

Mum and Dad have been together for 42 years. In many ways, they are an unlikely pairing, but you only have to see them together to understand the magic between them. They often comment that they'd be happy together at a bus stop. Dad says that he doesn't know who he is if he's not looking after someone – we all know what he really means is that he doesn't know who he is if he's not looking after Mum. She is the epicentre of his world and everything that he does within it.

Jess Mills

Mum grew up in the post-war dreich and rain of north-east Scotland. Her father was a respiratory doctor and her mother a radiologist who moved the family up to Aberdeen from London in 1952 when she was five. She grew up in a small, university-owned cottage that froze on the inside in winter – she would wake to a pitch-black morning, and watch her breath rise in icy blue clouds above her face. When she left home to go to university in Edinburgh at 17, she worked five jobs at a time until she became a social worker in her early twenties. She was elected as a Labour councillor in her mid-twenties and ran for election to become a Labour member of Parliament for the first time when she was 28. She is only five foot three, but she is a giant of a person. Her innate sense of responsibility for other people is likely the result of being the eldest sibling of three children, with parents who were often absent from home due to both their work and their barely functional alcoholism.

Now that I am an adult, I can see that her evangelical love of homemaking – seasonal flowers, pine-scented candles, quilts on sofas, the pleasure she gets from folding clothes away in immaculate piles in drawers lined with paper – is emotional. Having grown up with chaos and dysfunction, domestic order feels like safety and peace. Three months before Ottie was born, Mum announced her plans to redecorate Lower Farm to prepare for her arrival, in a performance of hoots and giddy, unapologetic laughter. 'Darling, Dad thinks I'm completely bonkers, but I just want it to be gorgeous for you when you come and to stay with the baby . . .' Endless discussions ensued over colour samples, how 'thrilled' she was with the choice to have 'cheeky monkey' patterned paper to line the baby's drawers. Her regular trips to John Lewis on Oxford Street between meetings to pick up more 'essential' items became accompanied by a running commentary. It was indulgence to the point of complete absurdity, but what pure and simple joy it gave us. She chose to redecorate my bedroom at Lower Farm in the same buttercup yellow that my room was painted when I was a child.

I now understand why she used to get so cross with me as a teenager for leaving a trail of mess behind me, and even more so for the fact that I didn't seem to realise I was doing it. 'Jessie! For god's sake, tidy up after yourself. When I was your age . . .' I hated feeling her disapproval. It made my palms flex hot. It felt both exposing and claustrophobic in the way that only her opinion of me can – and not because she was wrong, but because she was right. She never had the privilege of the feeling of security that provides space for the emergence of a selfish teenage disregard for others. Since she was a child, she has held everything, and everyone, together.

But the fact is, we are so different.

She's never said it to me explicitly, but I think she found the life I led for much of my younger adult life baffling. As soon as she graduated from university when she was 19, she started pursuing her work of public service. When I graduated from university, I pursued a career in music. I signed a record and publishing deal and then toured the world for much of my twenties. They were wild, very hedonistic years when I worked hard and played hard, in a perpetual tangle of best friends, boyfriends and all-night shenanigans. This period of my twenties coincided with the highest profile and most relentlessly demanding years of her career. Just before I left home, I would often be creeping in from a night out when she was already up and working at her desk: I could hear the low hum of Radio 4 and see the warm glow of the fire alight in her study reflected in the mirror as I tried to move silently up the stairway, unnoticed. Or I would turn up bleary-eyed for Sunday lunch with a blistering hangover when she had already done a full morning of campaigning in her constituency in south London. She would ask me, genuinely bewildered, 'But what on earth are you doing all that time into the small hours?' My dad would respond with raised eyebrows and snorts of knowing laughter. 'Oh Tessie, don't be so naive!'

I never doubted that she was proud of me back then because she told me often that she was, but these experiences never sat well with me. They made my life feel trivial next to hers of public purpose – because, in many ways, it was. She has always stood before me as a giant-sized example of another life, a different life, one that is charged with the fire of service to others.

❖ ❖ ❖

We drive round the final bend in the lane that leads to Lower Farm under a sky as black and still as a lake.

Everything has a strange patina of familiarity. I had been craving coming here, and yet I already know that arriving into the arms of my family won't provide that feeling of comfort and refuge that I wanted. I am feeling even more dislocated and unsettled than I did at our flat: intrusive and intimidating thoughts are pushing their faces up to the surface, inhaling oxygen, becoming fully alive.

I walk through the front door, with Finn's arms proud and wide around me and Ottie, and into the ebullient welcome of my mum, dad and brother Matthew. But I can't decipher what they are saying to me because suddenly the feeling of panic is pounding at my sternum. As I stand among them, I know I cannot explain this, so I say nothing about it and instead hear myself comment on 'the traffic coming out of London'. The grip of shame is neatly silencing me from telling them how I feel. Because how is it possible to tell anyone I am feeling anything other than simple joy and ease as a new mother, when every question that is directed at me is loaded with that assumption? How do I begin to tell them that I am drowning in catastrophic thoughts, when every look, interaction, either direct or indirect, with people I know or do not know, assumes entirely that my experience of new motherhood sits within the blandness of the linguistic container of 'happiness'? Instead, with Ottie held asleep at my chest, I am standing among my family, eyes now closed, with one foot upon the other, as if by touching less of this terrifying world we could be less within it.

As I stand there, Mum steps towards me as if climbing down from her watchtower to face me, and in moments we are walking upstairs through the cool and quiet air of the hallway, her arms draped around us like a cape, until we reach her room. She sits us on her bed and a bath is run. She undresses us both, then holds my arms at my elbows to steady me as I climb in and sit down into the warm lavender water and bubbles that rise and crackle around my stomach. At the curve of my neck, Ottie has woken with her tiny and powerful primal need. Her small downy head feels as tiny as a baby bird and she is arching her neck to find my breast. She begins screaming with an urgency that grabs at my insides like an assault. My heart is beating at my chest bone like a fish too long out of water. Quiet tears fill the base of my eye sockets, rising and overflowing like hot syrup until I can hear that I am crying, though it feels like vomiting, from a place within me that has no name.

Mum is sitting at the side of the bath and as I start to sob, her arms open wide to hold us both with the urgency of a reunion.

'Oh, my sweetest heart. I know. I know. It's OK, darling, it's OK . . . let's get you out.'

We are lifted out. Mum takes Ottie and wraps us both in warm towels.

She walks me one small step at a time to her bed. 'It's OK, my darlings, I'm here.'

She places Ottie in my arms again, her body still straight and rigid with primal need, her mouth frantic and searching to take in the part of me that is closest. Ottie finds my breast and in a moment, her body softens, her wide black eyes staring up into mine, bolting me back to the world.

◆ ◆ ◆

In the distance, the throaty morning call of a wood pigeon pierces the veil of sleep and I am lifted into consciousness. This is the sound of waking up from afternoon naps as a child. I inhale the air around my face – as it releases, it feels like a cool morning mist, rising to reveal sky again. My bedroom is in the eaves of the house with doll's house windows that open onto the one-track country lane that runs beneath us. A square halo is illuminating the blinds with an early morning sun that is blasting low beams across the west of England.

The past few days have been indistinguishable. I have been staring into a mind I don't know, a place where reason and rationality have been chewed apart by catastrophic thoughts. But right now, all that fills my senses through the distance of the walls and the flight of stairs between us is the cadence of Mum's voice in song. I raise myself to sit upright, my body stiff from days in hibernation. My eyes are thick with sleep. I walk onto the landing outside my room. 'The Skye Boat Song' is the song Mum sang to me most as a child; each turn of its melody is now rising up the stairs like a hand reaching out to me.

I take the stair rail in my hand to steady me, then start walking downstairs to the landing outside her room. Mum's bedroom door is ajar and I step into her room, blinking into the light. The windows are wide open, dazzling morning sunlight hitting Mum's bed where the two of them are laid. Ottie is splayed soundly upon her chest. Tight new buds of Mum's climbing rose are tapping at the window frame. I stand for a moment, taking them in, observing the confidence of instincts that suddenly I recognise, because they feel like my own. It is a moment of quiet recreation. They say that becoming a mother holds up a mirror, but now I know it is not just a mirror, it is a door to an entirely different world. Mum's eyes lift, poised to receive me. I walk round the bed and climb in through the cool side of the duvet to find their warm animal bodies.

She holds us both, on either side of her, in an embrace that surrounds us like a climate. Can you hear this heart? It beats beyond the page. Our bodies lie interwoven and generational like soft mountain ranges. Mum's arms squeeze tight and certain around us the way only hers can. 'My girls,' she says almost silently, like a prayer. Sun is beaming over our bodies, dancing long shadows and warm movements of renewed possibility across my eyelids.

◆ ◆ ◆

We Are Each Other

After two more weeks of convalescence, Finn, Ottie and I are leaving Lower Farm to drive across England to Norfolk to stay with Finn's mother, Nicolette. We spent this morning slowly packing up our room, Mum intermittently coming upstairs to tuck another new pyjama set or floral summer dress into Ottie's bag.

Before we go to the car, we walk round the garden together. Mum is picking us a posy of spring flowers to take with us. Ottie is asleep at my neck, sticky new leaves of the chestnut tree unfolding and hanging above us like green candelabras. At this time of year, Mum's garden is a symphony of heavy-headed peonies and sweet peas; the optimism she embodies is mirrored in the garden around us. Today, she picks us some of her coral peonies, dark purple and shocking pink sweet peas, yellow roses and some cow parsley from the lane. This image of her as she is now, with secateurs and freshly cut flowers in her arms, echoes some of my most vivid childhood memories – it is a timeless depiction of her.

I can see her twitching to stop herself from persuading us to stay longer.

'We'll be back in a couple of weeks, Mum.'

'I know, sweetheart. Ignore me, it's just – it's been heaven, hasn't it?' Her eyes sparkle at me.

'Yes, it has, Mum. It really has.'

The moments I will remember most from this time of navigating the gauntlet of postnatal anxiety are feeling the weight of her body on the side of the mattress next to me, the soft pads of her fingers stroking my head, the sound of her folding baby grows away in drawers, the sudden rush of water hitting the empty tub when yet another warm bath was being run.

I put Ottie in her car seat, shut the car doors, then turn to give Mum a hug goodbye, and she holds me with love that is huge and certain between us.

Everything I am has been made by what this love has given me. It is the home I hope I can give to Ottie, I think to myself, as I step back slightly so I can see her whole face and give her a kiss on the cheek.

'I love you, Mum.'

'I love you too, sweetheart. Now, drive safe, Finn darling, and let me know when you've arrived.'

As we drive round the bend in the lane away from

We Are Each Other

Lower Farm, I can see Mum standing in the front doorway behind us, both arms raised, her hands waving above her head, her face lifting into a smile. But, I can tell that her heart is in her mouth. It's an expression I haven't seen since I left for university when I was 19. As she disappears from sight, I can feel the arms and hands of separation are reaching, outstretched between us.

❖ ❖ ❖

Finn grew up under the widest skies in England, in Norfolk. The long, single-track lane that runs up to Nicolette's house is lined with the white lace of cow parsley and oak trees that are so old and wide, the bases of the trunks have started to meld with the adjacent oaks which were once a few metres away from them. Shimpling is a fifteenth-century Tudor house, one of the last true bastions of British bohemia.

Nicolette was born the same year as my mum. Her heart is as wide as the East Anglian coastal skies she grew up beneath. She is a timeless beauty of long, raven-black hair and legendary bohemian elegance. She has listening black eyes and strong hands that cut wood with an axe, but with warm and soft palms whenever she reaches over to touch my face with her characteristic warmth and affection. Her neck is adorned with heavy linked, silver Indian necklaces, one simple gold cross, the smell of Chanel No 5 and a woollen tartan scarf in winter. Her earlobes are decorated with woven gold hoops and odd silver studs. Each piece of jewellery holds its own story, a little gold or silver flag on the mountain of her life story. Finn inherited her aquiline features and her serenity. She is mother to Finn and his three siblings, but has spent her lifetime extending a mother's love to so, so many more. Nicolette is an artist who immortalises her family and friends in romantic, jewel-toned oil paintings. They hang off every inch of Shimpling's old timber walls, along its long, sloping corridors. They narrate a lifetime of motherhood, of seminal friendships, of loves and losses.

Shimpling is a place of both infamous parties and of sanctuary and refuge. Nicolette holds her door unconditionally open to her ever-expanding network of family and friends, who feel Shimpling is their own too. Shimpling has real magic, which feels at first like it is stored in the timber walls of its 500-year-old carcass. But really, it is manifested moment by moment by Nicolette, and her ability to make people feel that they belong. I am one of those people. We met shortly after Finn and I became an item in 2011 and it felt like being reunited with a lifelong friend. Now, of course, she is Ottie's grandmother too, which means that Ottie is held downstream at the point where the rivers of my mum's love and Nicolette's love combine. Ottie's birth has pulled us as close as people can ever be: now, we are all connected from the cells of our blood, in that place which is as encompassing as time.

We walk in through the rickety back door and, as the smell of Earl Grey tea, turps and woodsmoke hits the back of my throat, I feel my heart rate starting to slow. Nicolette's wide beaming smile and arms are reaching out to embrace us. Plates of Marmite on toast and cups of tea are already waiting on a tray by the fireplace.

Once we're assembled by the fire, I hand Ottie to Nicolette so I can get nappies from her change bag. I unzip the bag and at the top are presents for me that

Mum put in as a surprise. Some lavender bath oil, a pack of new knickers and a new white cotton dressing gown. 'Something for you too, darling.

Missing you already. I love you. Mum.'

◆ ◆ ◆

While Mum's garden is a symphony of peonies and sweet peas at this time of year, Nicolette's is all roses and lilacs. An arc of entwined blush pink roses and honeysuckle form an arch round the garden door, so when I walked out beneath them this morning, they released huge, perfumed petals and large droplets of dew onto mine and Ottie's cheeks.

Shimpling days turn in the shades of the immense sky. Today, the garden glistens under azure skies which soar over the susurrating oak trees, the protective walled garden, the 200-year-old sequoia tree and the ancient pastoral fields all around. When I was growing up, Dad would often say to us, 'It's one thing to have a nice time, it's another thing to know you are having a nice time.' This was a wonderful lesson in the gift of presence to impart to young minds, and with the wet, new leaves and carpets of primroses and crocuses all around me, the optimism and promise of spring has never felt so much like my own.

A new sense of lightness and confidence is emerging from that fragile darkness of the first weeks of new motherhood. I still feel this thread of connectivity to Mum which tugs sharply at my solar plexus each day, so we've been speaking most afternoons since I left Lower Farm. I've continued to notice that people don't naturally enquire as to how I am anymore. They ask how Ottie is. But Mum is still in the watchtower. When we're not together, she wants to know in precise detail how Ottie and I have both been since our last chat. Our conversations aren't 'about' anything; they are an ongoing stream of consciousness that narrates both the mundane and the profound. But within them lately there is that new dimension of celebration between us: new depths of intimacy, love and joy that are so tangible between us I feel I could throw my arms around them.

The air that is still and fresh at Shimpling is still and sweltering in London, and Mum is embarking on a full day of work that will take her to every corner of the city. She will turn 70 this autumn and we spent a good while this afternoon talking on the phone about what we should do to celebrate it.

'All I know, darling, is that if this is what 70 feels like then it's completely fabulous! Sweetheart, if I'm not finished up too late I'll call you on my way home so we can talk more. Otherwise, have a gorgeous day and let's speak tomorrow. Love to Finn and Nicolette and kiss my Otts for me. I love you, darling.'

'Love you too, Mum.'

When it is cloudless at sunset at Shimpling, light beams into the garden sharply from the west, striking the towering sequoia tree, and the garden becomes a stage – a flood-lit, melodrama of violet and tangerine light. By 6pm today, amid sparkling gin and tonics and the low murmur of Nicolette's radio, flutters of bliss fill the air. My heart, in this place, rises into steeples.

I discarded my phone on our rug in the shade in the long grass by the sequoia tree some hours ago, after our last chat with Mum. But as I'm standing here with Ottie asleep in my arms, something is agitating . . . from the shade of the other side of the garden I hear my phone ringing, and ringing. It had stopped but now it is ringing again. I walk over to the rug and

We Are Each Other

stand over it, watching it vibrating persistently with an unusual urgency. A 'no caller ID'. It's 6.42pm. Do the beginnings of a new world start in the soarings of the blood?

'Hello?'

'Hello, can I speak to Jess? This is Sergeant Phillips from Bishopsgate Police Station . . .' Then, a monstrous pause, which is latent with hesitation. I am as unprepared for the violence of the words then spoken as the deer is to the hunter as a bullet strikes its temple.

'Jess . . . I'm with your mum, at the Royal London Hospital . . . we need a next of kin to come to the hospital as soon as possible. She has had two large seizures and is unconscious. She is in a critical state. I'm so sorry. How soon can you or another family member get here?'

But I can't absorb what he is saying to me because adrenaline is cracking like forked lightning through all my vision and sounds. Ottie is in my arms, but I can't feel them and my legs are shaking. Our bodies are glowing in tangerine light from the sun which is still setting.

Jess Mills

Now my phone is convulsing with incoming calls that I answer to breathless voices: my brother Matthew, my dad, then the police again. Within moments, Nicolette is packing a bag for us and kissing our faces. Then the gravel of the driveway is under my bare feet and we are climbing into the car. And we are gone; the sound of the lane to Shimpling is beneath us as we drive entirely away from the idyll. Just the sound of my screaming internal prayer and the blood-black silhouettes of the Norfolk pines, surging past the windows like sideways gravity.

◆ ◆ ◆

As we drive into the concrete open-air car park at the Royal London Hospital in Whitechapel, it is aglow; sheets of biblical rain shatter against the floor into tiny amber jewels. Street lamps, skyscrapers and office blocks tower above. The city looks drenched in black silk.

I open the passenger seat door, leaving Finn to park the car with Ottie, and run, soaked instantly to my skin, to the back of the hospital. The doors to A&E slide open and the chill of the air conditioning makes my body prickle into goosebumps. A&E is full of people; the smell of sweet disinfectant and stress pheromones are so strong I can taste it.

I continue running, following signs marking the way through the hospital's brightly lit burrows of doorways and stairs that blur and swing around me, till I find the broad, sealed metal doors that mark the entrance to the emergency room. Eleanor and three of Mum's best friends are already there waiting for me. I arrive into Eleanor's arms, which are sprung wide and ready to gather me up. She holds me tight and steadies me against her because the edges of everything are moving. Matthew is travelling back to London on the sleeper train from Scotland that won't arrive till 5am. Annie and Luke are driving across town. Dad is on his way from Lower Farm.

As my sister is holding me, the doors to the emergency room part and a young strawberry blond doctor approaches me. His kind eyes meet mine and he asks me to come to one side.

'You must be Tessa's daughter, Jess?'

I can't render words into my mouth, so I nod.

'I've been looking after your mum since she

arrived. Some positive news – she is starting to regain consciousness.'

I breathe into myself so deeply that light pulsates at the edges of my vision. 'Please, tell me what's going on.'

'She has had two very large seizures and currently cannot formulate language. We need to identify what has caused the seizures. We think her symptoms are most consistent with a stroke so she is about to be transferred to the acute stroke ward so the registrar can observe her overnight. Jess, if you're ready, you can come and see her before she goes up.'

'Yes. Yes. Thank you.'

The emergency doors part, releasing strange noises, groans, bleepings and the quick steps of nurses and doctors attentive to the needs of patients in the row of cubicles. We walk the length of the emergency room towards a jade green paper curtain around the end cubicle, which is slightly parted. Before I see her, I see her shoes upturned on the floor, waiting there like an obedient dog.

The young doctor walks in ahead of me and pulls the curtain back. She is on her right side with her back to me. She is breathing deeply and restlessly; she is secured to the bed by thick, blue straps. Moving around to her side, I see that her eyes are closed and her face looks long. Her shoulders are rounded, her wedding ring is hanging right down her finger at her knuckle, the contents of her backpack are strewn on the floor beneath her. Her dress is cut from the neckline to her belly, with small blue pads and wires attached to the skin of her chest. She doesn't look like her.

I step cautiously closer, nervous to even move the air around her too much. I stand at the side of her bed, and my arms feel awkward at my sides so I lean in and put my face next to her cheek, my hands around hers. They are warm, gently responsive; her pulse is strong and regular just above her wrist. Her blood-red manicure that she got at the weekend is catching the light. As I feel each steady beat of her pulse rising to meet the pads of my fingers, a sense of relief starts to fill the space between everything.

'Mum? Mumma... It's me. I'm here, Mum, I'm here.'

I realise at this moment that I've never seen so plainly how entirely made of just only one mortal body she is. Because my mum is not just a person to me, she is a world. My words hover, suspended between us, and for a few moments she is unresponsive. Then, without moving, as she recognises my voice, she takes a long, deep breath into her nose – a breath which holds the power of the ocean, drawing the swell of shore-bound water into a wave. It awakens her hands and feet to flex. I don't believe in an omnipotent god, but I have been screaming my pleadings so loud into the universe that I imagine they may have been heard in unknown dimensions.

We stay in an embrace of stillness, my cheek next to hers, till I hear the rustlings of a young nurse coming to find me. 'Your boyfriend asked me to ask if you could come back to the waiting room because your baby needs feeding.'

As soon as the fact of Ottie's need comes into my head, my breasts harden, a surge of milk coursing like liquid glass through them. I stand next to Mum with my hands still on top of hers, with the front of my T-shirt now drenched, unable to let go of her. I feel ripped in two. I lean in to kiss her on her forehead, not knowing how else to leave, and rush back along the emergency room.

We Are Each Other

As the doors release, Ottie's frantic cry grabs at my insides and I pull her close into me. I'm entangled in my soaking T-shirt and bra and am trying to find my breast for her. Her eyes and mouth are screaming and searching for me. Milk is flowing in rivulets down my body and in the contours of Ottie's tiny facial features. I sit with my eyes closed, in an overwhelm of entanglement and separation. Eleanor doesn't say anything to me till Ottie starts to soothe and then, looking down at her in my arms, she puts her head of blonde curls to mine. The reassurance I need is not within reach, but she still tries.

'Oh, honey. I really think it will be OK.'

Is this how life changes? On this blue plastic seat in a cupboard-sized waiting room, with every part of me pushing against it?

I sit feeding Ottie till she is peaceful at last and sleeping again. It's 11.45pm and we are told to leave till the morning. Only my dad, who will arrive within the hour, can stay with Mum tonight. She should continue to stabilise, they say. I leave the emergency waiting room holding Ottie to me, Finn's arms wrapped around us, and we walk back through the hospital's winding tunnels, till we find the outside world again. It has stopped raining. The freshness of the city air hits my milk-soaked body like a cool mint spray. Heavy water droplets from the rainstorm that has just passed drip intermittently on my bare shoulders from trees lining the streets.

There is a small bird singing in the tree above our car. As I strap Ottie into her seat, it occurs to me that I've never questioned whether birds in song are singing or crying.

◆ ◆ ◆

I wake up to Ottie stirring next to me, with seams of yesterday's clothes pinching the skin at my waist and hips. I sit up in bed with a bolt of panic and scramble around the top of my bedside table to find my phone – the screen is full of messages and notification of a voicemail from Dad. My stomach twists into a knot. I pull Ottie closer into me, hold the phone to my ear. I cannot believe what I hear next. It's Mum.

'My sweetheart, it's Mum. Oh god. What on *earth* happened? I'm so sorry. I feel like I've woken up from a terrible nightmare but the doctor said it will be OK.

Call me as soon as you can. I love you. I love you, darling. Kiss my Otts for me. Call me on Dad's phone soon as you get this. Bye, darling.'

I listen to the message three times. I cannot believe it. I call Dad, who answers immediately.

'Argh, fucking hell. God, that was a fright. They think it was a stroke but are going to do a full MRI now just to confirm it. Mum's OK, she's come on a lot just in the last couple of hours. She's very confused and keeps getting cross with herself about it, but mainly because she can't remember the names of all the gorgeous nurses that are looking after her so beautifully, classic Mum. You must be knackered, darling, so don't rush. By some miracle, it looks like she's going to be OK.'

Within the hour, we're back at the sliding doors of the hospital, Finn is quiet and calm next to me. As the lift doors part to take us up to her, a scream-inducing feeling of relief lifts into my collarbones. The corridors on the fourth floor are empty and panelled in block colours of white and Kleinian blue. We arrive at the doors of the acute stroke ward, wait for a moment, then are buzzed through to the ward entrance, which is stuffy from unventilated morning sun. Dad is next to the drinks machine, waiting to take us through to Mum. I have never seen him without a clean shave in my life, so the 1 millimetre of hair on his face and the shrunken look of his frame immediately confirm what a hideous scare this has been for him too.

'Hello, darling.' He gives me a big hug and we stand for a few moments in an uncharacteristically long embrace. With his hand still at my back, we walk into Mum's room. She is propped up in her bed with starched white sheets neatly tucked in around her. As we walk into view, her arms rise up open and wide, and multiple different wires attached to her start flapping around her, knocking over a cup of water on her bedside table. I am unable to stop myself from bursting into tears of relief like I have never felt before.

'Oh, my girls, come here.'

She holds us in her arms and I start squeezing at her hands and fingertips as if to be completely sure she is still here. I feel like we have all just been saved from the entangled metal and glass of a near-fatal accident. A stroke is still serious, but with the evidence of recovery she has made just in the past eight hours, the

We Are Each Other

doctors have said with good rehab she should be back to normal life within a couple of months. Then we lie together, hands and fingers still squeezing into each other, with Ottie playing on our knees, till the late morning moves into the bustling delivery of hospital lunches on trays and endless cups of tea.

After lunch, Annie arrives, with bunches of peonies and some fresh pyjamas she picked up on her way for Mum. There is a quietly euphoric feeling that somehow, miraculously, the magic of our ordinary world is starting to resume.

As lunch is being cleared, we are planning family weekends at Lower Farm over the summer. Dad is performing to Mum's hoots of laughter in a hyperbole of opening and closing the windows to let the fresh air flush out the smell of incinerated hospital veg. Annie is arranging the peonies in a vase next to the bed and Mum is picking at a box of red velvet cupcakes, a dozen of which have just been delivered by a friend. The toll of the last 24 hours is hot in my eyes and, with Ottie now asleep on my breast, I am just entering the blissful glow of light sleep when there is a knock on the door.

An older male doctor with black rimmed glasses

and a clipboard comes in, followed a few paces behind by two others. Then he asks Mum if she would like us to leave the room.

'No, not at all,' she says. 'Why? Is everything OK?'

'Tessa, we have received your MRI results and . . .' He pauses and raises the scans up to the afternoon light of the window.

I look up to the black-and-white image of her skull hovering above us, like a noose for her neck. On the left of Mum's brain, there is a deep, black shadow the size of a golf ball.

Then, the doctor says words that spark white at the back of my head and bite down like the teeth of an animal on my back.

It wasn't a stroke, he says. She has cancer. She has cancer in her brain.

— *Summer 2017* —

I am at the kitchen window at Lower Farm, looking out over the garden.

Mum is sitting on her sun chair under the long, late-afternoon shadows of the silver birch tree. Translucent lime-coloured leaves are rustling under a searing blue sky. Ottie is in a bucket of warm water on the freshly mown grass next to her in a red-and-white-striped swimsuit Mum got her a few weeks ago. It is buttoned around her so she looks 'wrapped up', like an old-fashioned box of chocolates. The soft, rotating arch of the water sprinkler is igniting into momentary rainbows as it moves backwards and forwards through low beams of sun. Mum is singing to Ottie her self-proclaimed 'Ottie anthem' that she came up with spontaneously while giving her a bath a few weeks ago: 'You are a D-D-L-P perfect little bear . . . D-D-L-P stands for dearest, darling, little, precious.' The countryside is thrown around Lower Farm like a soft green quilt.

But everything feels still and silent, like a photograph.

It's been a week since Mum was discharged from hospital and, other than her feeling tired and being occasionally unsteady on her feet, it is so hard to believe that what happened at the Royal London was not just an awful dream.

But the doctors are sure. She has cancer in her brain, a large tumour, the size of a golf ball. They said it looks like an aggressive cancer because of how strongly the fluorescent pink dye she drank to prepare for the MRI scan illuminated it on the images. She will have brain surgery to try and remove as much of the tumour as possible. Then, tests will be done on it to determine her exact diagnosis. 'We don't know any more than that yet,' they said, laying out their words like pebbles along a wall. But the thing that is looping in my brain is not what they told us in words, but what I saw momentarily unveiled in the expression of the younger, blond doctor. He didn't speak much, but I could tell, in the split second when the mask fell away from his highly controlled expression, that he has seen the acid pink glow of this type of tumour on MRI scans before.

I haven't been able to control how every part of my being is still pushing against that look on the doctor's face – so much so that all my physicality is entirely raw. It's a feeling I have no other point of reference for. It has nothing to do with 'thinking' awful thoughts in my brain, or with the blandness of the language of 'shock' or 'anxiety'. This feeling is in the matter of my flesh. It is relentless and visceral, like having hair-thin razorblades pressed to my skin and veins.

We came back to Lower Farm with Mum, Dad and Matthew when Mum was discharged, and the bewildering mechanics of normality are going on all around me. Radio 4 fills the kitchen with the flow of the day's news at 7.30am while Dad makes coffee then eggs on toast. Then, the cycle of his signature meals are discussed and prepared. Dad came into the kitchen a few moments ago, looked under the sink and remarked on the need for more dishwasher tablets. Now, he's standing next to me, looking out the same window, not touching, to 'not' talk about it. We stand with just enough air between our upper arms, in silence, with the silent sensation of wailing rising from my chest into my throat.

It's impossible to truly know how you would respond to a situation like this as a family until you go through it, but I certainly wouldn't have thought this is how my family would deal with it. We talk about everything; nothing is ever hidden. Sometimes I wish things were more off limits. So it is completely unexpected that we just move around each other in the same mechanical way, not speaking about the fact that the unthinkable is happening to us. I feel strangely proud of this upright stoicism we are all showing to each other, but also confused by it.

Yet I do think I know why we keep moving each day to our normal rhythm – the alternative is to talk about what's happening. And ultimately, I *do not* want to talk about it, to make it even more real between us. Maybe we can't talk to each other because we are all individually consumed by the sensation of wailing inside our chests and throats, and talking about it makes the razors draw in so close to the skin it's unbearable. So all we *can* do is move our bodies through the day to the rhythm they are used to, to keep our eyes looking forward. Because if we meet each other's eyes, it might mean we see there is in fact a gun at all of our heads.

Each night since Mum was discharged, I have woken less than an hour after falling into an agitated sleep with Ottie still sleeping soundly next to me. My heart pounding hard and fast is the thing that wakes me, as if rousing from a bad dream, except what I now know is it's actually preparing me for waking, which is when this nightmare begins again. My stomach falls silently like a perfect stone through my mattress, that feeling of wailing begins and the razors lower to my skin. This continues throughout Ottie's next feed and while the thin, blue light of a bright, new summer morning backlights the window.

But last night I woke with the sensation of new matter in my body – a blackness in my veins that felt so inescapable and murderous that it terrified me to my bones. I climbed with quick steps from my bed into the bathroom next to our room and stared at my face in the mirror with all the lights on to check that I was still there. Ottie's blue and yellow bath toys were sunk to the bottom of an empty bath next to me, her red-and-white chocolate-box swimming suit hanging to dry on the radiator. Finn is exhausted at the moment and he was so sound asleep that I couldn't bring myself to wake him up, so I walked out of my room onto the landing and listened out, hoping I might hear signs that Matthew or Dad were awake too. The house was totally quiet around me. All I could hear was this ringing black silence and the faint tick tock of the grandfather clock two floors down. I felt something I've never felt before, in the epicentre of my family. I felt completely alone.

Mum's calling out to me now from the garden. 'Darling, I think Ottie's ready for her sleep.'

'OK, I'm coming, Mum.'

I carry out a tray with a pot of tea and slices of coffee cake and place it on the ground, then lift Ottie out of her bucket of water, which is cloudy with sun cream and has small, green blades of grass floating on

We Are Each Other

top. I wrap her up in a little towel with bear ears on it Mum got for her, and Mum raises her arms as a cue for a kiss and cuddles with her before we leave. 'Miss you already, Otts!'

I climb the stairs to our room, the one with the buttercup walls where two weeks ago, I was convalescing from birth in Mum's arms, the same room where those murderous things happened last night. I close the bedroom door and pull all the blinds down. There are two new pairs of pyjamas with flowers and little rabbits on them laid on the bed for Ottie from Mum. The sight of them makes my stomach clench to hold back tears that are already falling from my chin onto Ottie's head, forming patterns like raindrops in her swirls of stormy black hair. I don't want Ottie to see my face so I just hold her to my breast to soothe her to sleep. The clench of my stomach is now rising into a heaving sensation in my throat that feels like choking. I hold Ottie to me, rocking us back and forth like we are on a life raft, until she falls asleep, and I watch her jaw and soft mouth slow to stillness then release open, so now the only movement in her body is her chest rising soft and steady in deep sleep.

Jess Mills

I sit on our bed watching her sleep for a few minutes. Her body is already filling out the Moses basket that she was just a tiny dot in a few weeks ago. I walk downstairs, catching my reflection in the mirror on the landing as the front of the house is being blasted with low, late-afternoon sun. I stand for a moment so that the apricot coloured light warms my face on top of angry red blotches that are all over my cheeks and swollen eyes. My face looks both glowing and pummelled. I want to run so fast away from this that I could turn into wind, but I can't escape it because it is inside my life now.

I retrieve my sunglasses on the way back outside to the garden. I can hear Mum's secateurs snapping at the thick stems of her blousy coral pink peonies; the petals are so wide open now they look like they are gasping.

I walk recklessly straight over to Mum and stand right in front of her, to see if she is still in the watchtower.

She sits back down on her sun lounger, inviting me to lay down next to her. 'Did Otts go down OK, darling? I asked Dad to pick her up some new pyjamas from M&S, did you find them in your room? Such pretty ones, I thought you'd love them.'

'Thank you, Mum, they're gorgeous. I'll put her in them after her bath later.'

'Yes, let's do that, sweetheart. You're OK, aren't you, darling? What a perfect day. This was a perfect day. Wasn't it?'

The peonies are now laid on the grass, gasping beside us.

◆ ◆ ◆

We are back in London to prepare Mum for her surgery. With the balcony doors open at Mum and Dad's flat in north London, I can hear the ambient chatter of people filling cafés on street corners in the sunshine. But I feel like I am occupying life behind a pane of glass, bewildered by the feeling of complete separation, unable to touch normality.

To help manage the night terrors that have been perching on the end of my bed recently, in the evening, once Ottie is asleep, Finn has been helping to wade through endless research papers in medical journals in the hope that knowing this thing and what to expect better will somehow dispel its murderous and enigmatic exterior. I'm hoping that if I dare to gaze directly into that portentous look that I saw on that doctor's face, I will be more prepared for whatever may be behind it. But so far, all that we have been able to learn is that there are so many types of brain cancer that until Mum has her surgery and the tumour is analysed, we won't know which end of the spectrum she is at. One end is bad but manageable, at least for now; the other end is the stuff of nightmares, where the diagnosis is the death sentence.

What is clear to me, though, is that brain cancer doctors and neurosurgeons do something particularly sacred, because they are working in the epicentre of human identity. The job of the neurosurgeon is not just to protect the physical matter and biology of the brain, but the identity, the 'self', the 'being' of the patient. They are working in the place where consciousness and the most mystical parts of biology converge. When I think about it all too much, it makes everything move fast and slow at once, but we are nearly there now. Her bag is packed and ready by the bedroom door. But within it all, I am making

We Are Each Other

myself be hopeful, and I can already feel how hope is the antidote to despair.

◆ ◆ ◆

It is swelteringly hot. The windows of Mum's hospital room in central London are pushed open the few inches they will reach. Ottie is at my breast, the bare skin of our stomachs sticky with sweat now she is stripped down to just her nappy, after being too hot and bothered clothed. Dad is sitting on a seat next to Mum's hospital bed, and Finn and Matthew have just returned with some cold drinks.

Just after 4pm, the surgeon comes in. We all adjust ourselves to sit further upright in our seats. Mum reaches out her hand with characteristic warmth and focus to shake his. He introduces himself with a friendliness that quickly moves to pragmatism as he goes on to describe the next steps and the likely outcomes.

Before he finishes, he pauses, then adds, 'You also need to be aware that this operation is potentially not curative, but it will lead to a clear diagnosis. This is the beginning of a journey. And today, before the surgery, Tessa, you will need to make some important decisions.'

Mum's tumour is on the left side of her brain, just above her ear, which is the cortex that controls speech and language. I have seen it written again and again in the research papers and books Finn and I are wading through that, from a neurosurgical perspective, these are considered the most sacrosanct regions of the brain.

'Damage to these areas through surgery or through the invasive growth of inoperable tumours can result in the inability to understand, speak or write language. Even if a person may be able to form the motor function of words, they have no coherence – their words are produced as a flow of incoherent sentences, disconnected words and grammar with-out semantics,' the surgeon says.

I read just last night that if a combination of some or all of these things happen, it could be so obliterative to Mum's sense of identity and ability to connect and commune with the rest of the world that, even if she survives, it's common that people then die, as if by will, much sooner than may be anticipated. For what kind of life exists without the possibility of communication? Without it, she could become her own prison.

Professionally, her gift for communication is how she became one of the most authentic and respected politicians of her generation. Personally, it is also how the purest and most glorious parts of her are expressed – her emotional intelligence, her enthusiasm, her sense of humour and how she conveys love. To ensure she is kept alive for as long as possible, will we risk her paying the price of having the crucible of her identity destroyed? The responsibility we have now, as her family, is not just to fight for her survival, but to fight for it only as long as the life she will have left will be one that is worth living.

So the question we need to answer, as the nurses are bringing round cups of afternoon tea and digestive biscuits, and Ottie is rooting round my chest to be fed again, is, knowing all the risks, do we want him to try to remove it all completely? The surgeon says that in order to do so, he will have only a 1 millimetre margin for error. Completely removing the tumour will increase her chances of longer survival, but 1 millimetre to the left could render her a different person.

Jess Mills

As the surgeon is talking us through the other possible risks, Mum sits up in her bed and starts speaking. I realise the whole time he has been here, she has been standing on the cliff edge, preparing to take the leap. She says to him, but while looking directly at me, 'I want to try and get it all out.'

There is a pause where I try to speak and I don't; instead, my stomach twists into a grey knot with immediate shame that I am not brave enough to put the question back to her, so she feels the permission to make this decision free from our need as her family for her to be alive as long as possible for us. As the pause extends into prolonged silence between us, her eyes lift into a smile.

Eventually Dad speaks. 'Are you sure that's what you want, darling?'

'Yes, it's my decision. It's what I want,' she says, still looking at me.

◆ ◆ ◆

Before we leave the hospital for the night, Mum suggests we go for dinner at a little Italian restaurant around the corner, where, in our former life, we have had many happy times as a family knocking back red wine and negronis and spaghetti Bolognese. We are greeted by the waiters with their usual theatrical charm, as if it was just another normal family supper. And, in many ways, it is. Everything and nothing has changed. Dad orders the wine; Mum orders a salad for her and chips for the table, which she eats most of. The chatter from the tables around us softens the edges on the uncharacteristic long pauses of silence between us. Conversation rises up occasionally like a buoy, something to hold onto.

When Mum leans in towards me and starts talking, I have to move closer because she's speaking quietly. The toll of the day is showing in her face, in the way she is blinking slowly. As the waiter is reaching over our shoulders, serving small plates of calamari and Caprese salad, and the red wine bottle is clinking on our eager, empty glasses, she locks eyes with me from the watchtower for the first time since her seizure: 'Darling, if I didn't wake up tomorrow, you know there is nothing else we need to say to each other, don't you?'

My brain flinches and I want to tell her not to say it – but before the words come out, she rests her hand on top of mine and repeats herself. I let her speak. She says, 'There is nothing else we need to do, nothing else we need to say, darling.' There is no fear in her eyes. In the noise and clatter of the Italian restaurant, her words stay suspended in the air between us and suddenly I realise what she is doing: she is handing me a gift. Then as she takes my hands, squeezing my fingers and palms in a way that only she does, I look towards this thing which feels so completely Other: Death.

Whenever I have tried to turn my mind to the possibility of her death, my brain and my thoughts have flinched – but for this moment, I feel completely suspended in the air, unearthed and disconnected from the ground, and something very uncomplicated and simple appears to me. That if these were our last moments, just sitting here with our hands clasped, she's right: there is *nothing* unsaid, *nothing* unresolved between us. And then I feel something I haven't felt till now, and it rises in my chest. I feel brave. So I step forward and leap from the edge of my fear to let the possibility of her death enter my brain. And in this moment, my face as wet as a newborn, it only makes us more real.

We Are Each Other

Ottie wriggles forward on my knees and reaches for the crust of a baguette.

'Oh, look, darling . . .' Mum's face lights up. 'She loves that, doesn't she?'

❖ ❖ ❖

Being midsummer, on my way home from saying our goodbyes at the hospital, the sun has not quite set over London. I turn into my road and I pull into a space next to a grey painted wall, where overnight someone has graffitied: 'Because You Are Alive Everything Is Possible'.

I don't believe in an omnipotent god but I am aware that since Mum's seizure, I have started to search for, or at least opened my mind to, the possibility of a higher order. I know I am searching for these things because I need them, but finding these words on this street corner doesn't feel coincidental. It is as if they have been written for me to discover on this exact journey home today. As I stop the car the heavens open; summer rain falls as if the skies are sobbing.

❖ ❖ ❖

My phone vibrates on the bedside table next to me. Matthew stayed with Mum last night in the chair next to her bed so he could take her down to her surgery in the morning.

'She's out of surgery,' he says. His voice is quiet yet soaring with relief.

Her surgeon is 'delighted' with the surgery, Matthew says. He managed to remove the whole tumour with an entirely clean margin. We now need to wait for the tumour to be analysed so we can receive her full diagnosis, but, 'We couldn't have hoped for a better outcome at this stage,' the surgeon has said. It means the mass of the tumour is out of her brain and her soul is still intact. It means she's coming home.

◆ ◆ ◆

Just a week after surgery, Mum is able to walk only lightly supported by Dad's arm through the light and airy lobby of this huge cancer centre in central London to meet her oncologist and receive the official diagnosis and prognosis. We follow directions to a waiting room in the basement for this meeting that all moments since her seizure have been building up to. We wait to be seen on hard, black plastic seats outside the consultation room for nearly an hour. Mum is very tired today. She spends most of the time we are in the waiting room nodding in and out of sleep on my right shoulder. Ottie is asleep at the crook of my neck on my left.

Eventually her name is called. Mum walks in ahead of Dad, Matthew, me and Ottie, who's still asleep. Mum is poised and silent. In the brilliant white of the consultation room her skin looks golden after all our time in the garden these past few weeks. But belying her composure, above the collar of her pale blue cotton shirt, the pulse at the top of her neck is beating hard and fast, I notice.

Mum, Dad and Matthew sit down. Dad sits next to Mum and keeps looking at the floor. I stay standing, swaying side to side, trying to keep Ottie asleep at my neck. My heart is beating so loud into my ears that when the oncologist introduces himself I can't hear what he said. He is middle-aged, pale-skinned with black-rimmed glasses and sandy brown hair, he is wearing black leather lace-up shoes. The left lace is undone. He opens his file and starts turning pages of his notes. We are obedient, quiet and still.

I don't know what I expected this moment to feel like, but even before he starts talking, I'm aware I don't have a frame of reference. There is a clear and chilling dissonance to the way he is going through the formalities of behaving in an ordinary manner, and yet I can already tell: he is reaching into Mum's hospital notes for a fully loaded gun.

As only the white lights of the consultation room hum above us, I cannot tell you that I knew what was coming because I didn't. Even if I had known the facts of it, I never could have anticipated how the knowledge of it would feel inside my body.

He starts speaking – but not with words, with the cruelty of fire, which moves over the cries of what it burns. All I can hear is *ten to 13 months*. The words on the page we are handed say this too, though I can't read them because they have entered my brain like hot teeth biting down at the back of my skull and my eyes can't focus on the page.

'Glioblastoma is the most common primary brain tumour, and one of the most aggressive types of all cancers. Even with maximum treatment, the cancer always recurs. The average survival following diagnosis is ten to 13 months. Without treatment, survival is typically three months.'

'Yes, you have had a successful surgery. But this type of cancer can never be fully extracted by surgery and cannot be cured. Tessa, even though the main tumour mass has been removed, your scans show that the cancer cells have already diffused extensively into the middle of your brain, so it will return. It's just a matter of when, not if.'

He pauses. Then it starts again.

'Unfortunately, we have found a particularly aggressive gene in your cancer which means chemotherapy is unlikely to work, so it is up to you whether you would like to pursue that, but you are still able to have radiotherapy. That is it. I'm afraid we have no other treatment options to offer you.'

We say nothing because none of us are able to speak. I am still rocking Ottie side to side and all I can see are Mum and Dad's hands and fingers squeezing into each other. Mum's skin has risen into a red flush; her bright blue eyes look like they are trembling. She turns to me with a stare that fixes on me and Ottie. The doctor starts speaking to her again, but she doesn't look at him. She continues looking past him and straight at us. I can't hear what he is saying now because all I can see is her face and eyes mouthing the words: 'I love you. I love you.' She looks so real it is like her edges have been drawn in in a thick, black marker pen.

Then, a nurse, who I hadn't realised had been standing at the back of the room the whole time, starts talking. She says we should call her tomorrow because it's normal to need time to process this news. She imagines we will have lots of questions and we need to make a plan for Mum to start her treatment.

We leave the consultation room in silence, climb the stairs to the entry hall and walk out of the hospital, Mum leaning on Dad's arm as she had done when we arrived. We go out through the revolving glass doors not looking at each other, not speaking, into the roaring traffic and noise of Tottenham Court Road. Buses, people laughing on their mobile phones, the vendor selling London souvenirs on the street corner in the same spot as he was when we arrived.

We climb into the back of a black taxi. Dad's phone starts ringing – it's Luke calling to see how the appointment went. Dad says he'll call him back as soon as we get home. I can tell he can't bear to say it out loud because doing so will make it more real. I reach for Mum's hand, our fingers pushing into each other.

'Whatever this is, darlings, we can do it,' she says, as if this is happening to us, not to her. My only framework for a nightmare so far in my life has been one I could wake up from. But this is a nightmare that no one can end now.

The taxi drops us off at the gate to her flat, its metal carcass purring off down the hill as Matthew reaches into Mum's bag for her door keys. Dad turns and walks a few steps away so he is standing with his back to us; he is bent over slightly as if he might be sick. Then his shoulders involuntarily rise to his ears, the back of his body shaking. He is crying. I've never seen my dad cry. I understand, in the pit of my stomach, that the way we each love Mum, the way we each feel that she is our home, is now the noose for our necks.

◆ ◆ ◆

I've just received a message from a former colleague who had a baby a few days before me: 'How are you, lovely? Sorry for not being in touch, it has been nonstop with the little one! How's new motherhood treating you? Let's catch up with the babies soon.'

I start typing. 'Hi love. It's nice to hear from you. It's a hard one to answer, really. Ottie feels completely miraculous but things are not so good. My mum has been diagnosed with terminal brain cancer. To be honest, I'm just putting one foot in front of the other, with my mum in one arm and Ottie in the other.'

Then I stop. I delete what I've written. Because how can I explain to someone outside of this what is really going on? What can I say? I feel I am both inserted into new motherhood and completely outside of it. Everything is a paradox. I could tell her I have become severed from the real world and I cannot find the way to break back into it again, or anywhere to take refuge, least of all inside myself because I have no feeling of separation between my insides and what is exterior. No membrane. I am porous.

Or that I have no idea what a 'baby bubble' feels like because at the moment, I'm existing on a mainline of adrenaline which is doing its work, chiselling new capacities in my body for despair, courage and love.

Or maybe I should comment on the weather?

How the sun is shining perpetually in England this summer, but that there is this deathly dark and murderous thing growing like a black triffid within and between everything.

Shall I remark that I have heard accounts of people going through similar things, caring for a gravely ill loved one, or living through the shock and horror of a sudden death, who have shown such grace and poise? But I do not feel like that. I feel so, so many ugly and awful things – jealousy, rage, helplessness and just this throbbing, merciless sadness that this is happening to her, to us – that is occasionally so vicious it makes my stomach clench so that I involuntarily let out a small moan from my mouth, which sounds like an animal in pain.

Or shall I tell her that I feel such shame? That somehow I should be, like other people seem to be, 'dealing with it' better? The only comfort is that most of the time, no one knows. When Ottie reaches her arms up to me, I find I can pat myself together like a mound of dry sand. So I am there, both crumbling and held together, hopefully just enough to raise a smile, which makes my mouth part like a cut.

Now it occurs to me — maybe that's what was happening for those other people who I thought were dealing with their own tragedies with that poise and grace. How extraordinary, I think, that human beings can smile with their faces while their bodies on the inside are in a furnace. Fuck. Where have I gone? Who the fuck am I now?

I won't write back that it's only 1pm and I already want a glass of wine. Not because it's a glistening early summer afternoon or because I'm about to meet friends to start the weekend early, but because I love the way it loosens the grip around my stomach and blurs the edges of my thoughts for a while, until all I want to do is turn up the radio a little and dance in the kitchen for a moment with Ottie on my hip. She loves it. She loves seeing me smile and dance, and a glass of wine helps me keep that mauling sadness locked up till it breaks its chains again.

Probably better to write back another time.

❖ ❖ ❖

I read an article this morning about something called 'psychogenic syndrome'. This is caused by an electrical short in the brain, triggered by the shock of the news of a terminal diagnosis for you or a loved one. In some cases, it means the brain shuts down completely and the person falls into a psychogenic coma. The treatment of this syndrome consists, simply, of speaking reassuringly until words connect and they awaken. Hearing this felt like a relief because it explained to me the cognitive violence of the experience in that consultation room.

The plainest horror of it, from which my brain and body startles – I am just two hot eyes. I cannot accept it. I cannot even think of it. When I think about it, a small detonation happens behind my eyelids.

❖ ❖ ❖

I can't stop taking photos and videos of us all together. Preserving our bodies, breathing and alive together. But in doing so I am also aware that I am changing her, already rendering her as a memory.

Yet I also need to know that these moments that we are inserted in, alive together, have been accounted for, and recording them in this way is the only way I have to do that.

Jess Mills

It is an ongoing act of love.

◆ ◆ ◆

Mum is standing at her bathroom mirror. Her head is tilted, slightly turned to one side as she moves her fingers along the bare skin of her head. Her hairstyle and colour are a marker of time. Looking at any photograph of her, I can tell exactly what era it was by her haircut and colour alone – her naturally dark, chocolate brown Joan of Arc-style bob of the late seventies and early eighties evolved to an auburn crop in the late eighties, to a caramel bob in the 1990s then back to a longer, auburn crop with some highlights in the 2000s, to a golden caramel crop with highlights, which she had the day she collapsed with the seizure.

I remember looking at her hair as she lay in the recovery room at the Royal London Hospital and feeling struck by how well styled it looked while the rest of her body was slumped, her face long. She's always coloured it and never had any visible grey hair, even at her roots. For the first time in my life, right now, I can see grey hairs creating a thick, silvery bed across on her scalp. She has such vivid blue eyes that the halo of grey makes her eyes look like a bright summer sky next to the metallic grey tones of the sea.

The radiotherapy damages hair follicles, so the area she's been receiving treatment on is now almost bald. She runs her fingers through the longer hair on the crown of her head, then pauses cautiously, with curiosity, to touch the few remaining longer fuzzy strands of hair that remain on the left side of her head above her ear. I'm sitting on her bed; Ottie's thickening and chubby body is asleep at my chest. Instinctively mirroring Mum, I run my fingers through Ottie's chocolatey brown hair, which is now thick between my fingers and more than an inch long all over her head.

Mum is two weeks into her course of radio and chemotherapy. Every day, she takes a pill called temozolomide. We have been told, because of the very aggressive subtype of cancer she has, that it won't have much benefit for her at all, but it's all they can offer. 'It may extend your life by a few weeks,' they said, as if it were just any other matter of business. Each time Mum is told that something is 'all they can do', I see impatience and disbelief rise in her expression.

Jess Mills

It is absolutely typical of her that every day this week when she has returned from hospital where they have applied radiation to the area above her ear where the tumour was, and where its feathery tendrils are still alive, burying deeper into her brain, she has had the familiar fire of injustice in her eyes, which I have seen in her often throughout my life. Today, for the first time since this all began, she came home in tears – because she had been sitting in the waiting room next to an 18-year-old boy who, last week, was also handed his death sentence. He was told 'there was nothing else they could do' for him too.

'He was sitting there waiting for his radiation with his lovely dad. I just cannot bear it,' she said, cup of tea in hand, her voice choking slightly, eyes staring into the middle distance, her hair thin and tufty above her ear on the left of her head.

She looks like she has cancer now. The local greengrocer yesterday, noticing her thinning hair, asked, 'Everything OK, Tess?' Having tried initially to keep the truth of what is happening limited to a small group of Mum's friends, the grip on the news has loosened and people know; I think everyone knows now. So for each of the past few days that we've all been in London, a different friend of Mum's has been arriving with keen, concerned eyes, punctual at Dad's designated visiting time of 3pm, with flowers, cakes and offerings of love, to listen to Mum's outrage at how archaic the treatment options are for her and all the patients she's been meeting in the radiotherapy waiting room. Then they leave, stunned, with a new clarity on the situation and yet still a look of disbelief in their eyes as I walk them to the door, often while they are still saying their elongated goodbyes to Mum, who calls out from the top of the stairs with her typical ebullience – 'Thank you for the gorgeous flowers, it was heaven to see you, love to Will, have a wonderful holiday, let's make another plan soon!' Then once out of Mum's earshot, they turn blankly to me and say: 'She will be OK, Jessie, won't she?' I don't know what to say to them, so I just try to lift a smile and tell them to come and see us soon.

Today, it was Georgia, Mum's friend and colleague of almost 30 years. Ottie and I stand at the front door as usual, waving with a smile, going through the requisite performance she needs from us as she walks to the road and is released from this. As she reaches the pavement, I see her pause, breathe a deep sigh and reach for her mobile phone, maybe to call her husband who couldn't come with her today because of work commitments. It is a Tuesday after all; everywhere around us normal life is marching on. In our previous life, it would have been unheard of for Mum to be at home mid-afternoon during the working week. I heard her say she was 'unsure' if she would 'be back to work as usual' to Georgia just now. It's the first time I've heard her refer to the future in this way. She said it so plainly, completely devoid of self-pity or pathos. I know it was startling for us all to hear it out loud.

I'm certain Georgia will now be telling her husband it's much worse than she had thought and that they must remember to keep checking in as she walks along the row of houses and quickly out of sight. By now, she has probably changed the subject of their conversation to their plans for later this evening, what's for dinner, how their children are today and how they can't wait to go on the holiday she just told us about to Mallorca this weekend. By the time she gets into her car and starts the ignition, the normality of her world will have resumed – because what is happening is merely a temporary agitation in a far corner of the surface of their lives, which are otherwise still entirely intact. But we don't have an outside world anymore. Everything is locked inside this world, where black triffids grow up the kitchen wall during a quiet, sunny breakfast and eyes sparkle with sadness over cups of afternoon tea.

I walk back inside and over to Mum, sitting on the sofa. Afternoon light flickers across her legs. Ottie is on her lap, giggling, grabbing at her lips and sucking on her chin as Mum sings 'The Skye Boat Song' to her on repeat. It's Ottie's favourite song now too.

She is right here in front of me, yet I am missing her so much my stomach clenches and that small noise, like an animal in pain, involuntarily came out of my mouth again. So I stand up to turn my back, and quickly and calmly walk to the kitchen. I turn the kettle on and open and close the kitchen cupboards a few times as if I was just coming over here to make tea, so she and Dad won't hear it, if it happens again.

As the kettle boils, Dad comes into the kitchen to start bringing out the dinner that he's already prepared. It's only 5.30pm but Mum is ready for bed by 7.30pm at the moment so we've been eating dinner early. Dad hasn't left Mum's side since her seizure. Observing the quiet purity of his devotion to her makes my heart both lift and break, at once. His greatest love and his greatest heartbreak are now spinning on the same wheel. It was Dad who first told me 'cooking is an act of love', which is apt because it is one of the ways his love for us all has been interwoven into our day to day our whole lives. His peeled cucumbers in salads, finely chopped chives on grilled summer chickens, pick your own raspberries and cream with homemade meringues.

Though now, Dad's delicious pastas and Mum's favourite stews with mashed potatoes have been replaced with a low-carb, no-sugar meal from one of the many 'diet vs cancer' books which line the kitchen tops and that Dad loathes. We all eat these meals together in solidarity, but Mum really only picks at them.

This evening, we sit down with the balcony doors wide open, Dad's classical music playing on the radio. Green salad and white fish, with a rainbow plate of raw vegetables all peeled and cut for her. Dad and I are hungry, so eat it all up till our plates are clean and empty. But Mum's plate looks even more full when she's finished than when she started. After ten minutes or so without touching anything, she looks at Dad, and squeezes his hand and says, 'Thank you, darling, that was delicious. I'll manage to eat more tomorrow, I think.'

Dad leans and kisses her on her cheek, then gets up and walks to the kitchen, lifts the lid off the bin without saying a word and scrapes the uneaten food off her plate. It feels like watching him get whipped.

❖ ❖ ❖

For the first time in weeks I am not astonished awake.

One lone beam of golden morning light has broken in through the crack in the curtains and is cast across the duvet as if it was sent to search for me. I lift my arm and I extend my hand to it, watching the light fall between my fingers.

A cooled cup of tea is on the bedside table that Finn must've brought up while I was asleep, along with a note: 'Just popped out to the shops, call me when you wake up. Love you.' Everything is quiet downstairs.

There is only the soft purr of car engines and the chatter of people from the street outside.

Mum and Dad are seeing friends today, so I have made no plans. In the context of the past weeks, having time alone with Ottie at home, with nothing else to do, is novel. This is the first time since Mum was diagnosed that I can feel the motion of my day following a more ordinary flow of what it must be like for most other people who have a new baby. A tangle of Finn, mine and Ottie's clothes from yesterday are jumbled on the floor. Baby grows are knotted in the legs of my jeans and her baby monitor is blinking its full battery bars at me. The feeling that everything is happening too late or too early, the rest of the day wide open, unpunctuated with plans, like a prairie.

Ottie is still curled up on her side next to me. Sleeping together like this with her makes me feel like an animal. Everything about it feels like nature's most distilled capacity for nurture and protection. I sit up in bed and, even though she is just next to me, she still feels too far away, so I lift her still sleeping onto my chest and pull her in closer to me, like a child with a teddy bear.

We Are Each Other

A card from Mum to me, dated 14.02.17, two weeks before Ottie was born, is still on my chest of drawers. How strange it is that so often when the world changes, it does so on our insides so no one else can see.

My phone vibrates on the bedside table next to me. 'Mum', the phone screen blinks. It surprises me. I realise as I answer the phone that this is the first time she's called, from her own phone, like she used to every day, since her seizure.

'Mum?!'

'Hello, sweetheart. Everything OK, darling?' Her voice for a moment sounds as though none of this has ever happened. Through the phone, she sounds normal and strong. 'Darling, I woke up today worrying about you – you didn't look yourself yesterday. Are you OK?'

My thoughts feel like arms trying to move in a straitjacket, so for a number of seconds, I can't reach for anything to say back to her, and we sit on each end of the phone together in silence.

'Sweetheart, are you there?'

— *Autumn 2017* —

Finn and I got together back when my life was much simpler, when I lived in a perpetual entanglement of late nights with friends. On the particular night I met Finn, I walked through the front door of my best friend's house at 2am holding heavy plastic bags clattering with beers and bottles of vodka and tonic. Through the haze of cigarette smoke, music, chatter and swaying bodies, from the other side of the living room, his face appeared – the friend of a mutual friend. Within moments of my arrival, he was standing in front of me, being introduced for the first time, and my whole being reacted in a way that was exact and gravitational. I was struck by a feeling I'd never had before: that I had never seen someone who was as beautiful as him in real life, with his enigmatic, quick-witted intelligence.

We talked and talked, the muscles in his arm shifting, occasionally averting our eyes, till the music went off, cigarette smoke clung to the living room ceiling and the low-hanging clouds outside the windows lifted with early morning sun. Every day for a year after that first meeting, up until we became lovers six years ago, I yearned for him in a way that felt like homesickness. It was during our first date that I experienced something I had never imagined until then: the feeling of wanting to belong to someone, completely and utterly.

The stillness of certainty is a particular kind of heaven.

Mine and Finn's relationship has never been an experience of tearing down all our boundaries; I am the guardian of his space, and he is the guardian of mine. There is the rare feeling between us of having both intimacy and tremendous expanse. But this momentous year, as we have been walking the frontier of new parenthood and the vortex of Mum's diagnosis together, we have had less capacity to be present for each other than at any other time in our relationship. Yet I can feel that our roots are now even more entwined, deep below the earth. Even though we are in the trenches of life together at the moment, being with him makes me feel free.

We are all back at Lower Farm to make the most of a long weekend between Mum's hospital appointments. The sound of Luke's laughter in the kitchen with Dad, the sight of Annie at the end of the sofa massaging Mum's feet, Eleanor arriving with coffee cake for tea and Matthew laid out on the sofa watching football create a simulation of our life as it was. For a few hours, it feels like the distance between the past and the present has closed a little.

While we were sitting round the kitchen table this morning, eating eggs and bacon, Finn suggested that he, Ottie and me go out for dinner this evening to celebrate our sixth anniversary, which is today. It felt like a radical act, for him to suggest, and then for me to agree, to do something so part of normal life, like momentarily crossing the road to walk in the sunshine for a few hours. 'I'm going to book a table early so Ottie can come with us too,' he said.

Jess Mills

As we drive round past the front of the house, to my surprise Mum is standing in the doorway to wave us off, hands raised, blowing us a kiss in the rearview mirror.

Our local pub is a seventeenth-century inn with low-beamed ceilings, sloping old flagstone floors and open fires. The bell over the main door into the bar has jangled exactly the same way over my head every time I've come here throughout my life. I love it here. It feels steeped in the ages, and I often think about the lives and conversations over the last four centuries that have played out around the bar.

Finn has booked us a table on the big chairs by the fire. It's a tonic to have some time away from Lower Farm. Even when the house was full with the bustle of all of my siblings today, it remained saturated in so much unarticulated sadness between us all. I often don't realise how I am choking on it until I step away from the house for a few hours into the world beyond it. We sit down and my phone lights up on the table between us with a message from Nicolette: 'Thinking of you, darling one, how are you and my Ottie? Shimpling is missing you and so am I. Shall I come down and see you in London next week to help you and Finn with Ottie? I love you, your Nicky.'

I pick up my phone to message back right away – the prospect of time with her in London feels like the ultimate balm. As I start typing, Finn reaches his hand across the table to take mine and says, 'Whatever happens, it will be OK. You will be OK, do you know that?'

My instant reaction to this is a wretched and irritable defensiveness, but I manage to bite my tongue just in time, because by looking at his face I can see the purity of intention of someone who thought they were handing me a gift. And, in fact, he has. As I focus on these words, for the first time all the possibilities that my life could still hold, of so much that is beautiful and good that could endure beyond the inevitability of Mum's death, appear to me and it lifts my sight to a different horizon, where a chink of light has suddenly appeared.

I can see Finn feels lighter for being away from Lower Farm too. Ottie is curled up on his lap, so content, her eyes bright black and ignited by her search for crusts of bread that she grabs at then chews till they start to disintegrate in her mouth and fall on Finn's lap. Just sitting here opposite one another, talking to each other and not talking about Mum for a while, it strikes me that while I am unrecognisable to myself at the moment, I could have also become unrecognisable to him. It's a feeling that makes me want to pull him as close into my body as possible, and so I get up and walk round the table and sit on his other knee, and we sit there by the fire, my arms round them both until the waitress brings us our food.

The bell jangles above our heads again as we walk out into the night. It is inky black and cold. The sweet decay of rotting leaves and woodsmoke from the fireplaces that are aglow in cottages lining the tiny village green hits the back of my nose and throat. This combination of smells in the countryside in autumn is as enduring as time itself.

We step out into the darker silence around the pub and Finn starts to walk in the opposite direction to the car, towards an ancient circle of oak trees in a small, dimly lit enclosure in the middle of the village. I'm not ready to go back yet. I want the night to carry on so I follow him. The moon is as bright as a promise in the sky and the bare branches of the oaks are illuminated above us, like arms, hands and fingers reaching up to the stars. Finn stops in the middle then turns to face me. I am unsure as to why he is lowering down, now onto his knees, until his and Ottie's black eyes are staring up at me and he says, 'I love you, darling, with all I am. Will you marry me?'

My siblings have each had to leave for London before we return so we arrive home to just Mum and Dad's keen and elated faces. Finn had told them he was going to propose this morning before we'd had eggs and bacon. They are waiting at the back door with a bottle of champagne ready. We drink a glass together, then Dad takes Mum to bed and we call Nicolette. Finn tells her the news and her voice erupts in cheer then a choke of raw emotion. She tells us how much she's missed our regular trips to Shimpling over the summer; I tell her I have too, so much. She offers to host the wedding party at Shimpling. I tell her I love her and I can't think of anything more perfect.

Finn and I stay up and drink together till the rest of the house is asleep, then we move into the bathroom and, under the brightness of the bathroom light, where nothing can be hidden, he undresses me and my clothes fall to the floor like bandages.

◆ ◆ ◆

Last night, wild autumn winds wailed through London's streets and trees, shaking the windows and front door of our flat with a low and furious force. Now the thin light of morning is glowing behind the curtains, so I reach from my side of the bed to pull them back and survey the scene outside: a slowing, swirling sky which is the colour of bruises, and small branches and debris from the contents of residential bins strewn along the street and the pavement.

I turn under the duvet to face Ottie and Finn, who are still fast asleep next to me. Ottie has slept so soundly that she didn't wake for her usual feeds, so I've woken up with throbbing breasts that are as hard as rock at the sides and starting to leak into my nightshirt. There's something so rare about this moment of peace, in which nothing is being asked of me, that I lie still until the throbbing becomes sharp and painful, then get up and walk quickly with light steps downstairs, trying not to wake them.

We Are Each Other

Once in the kitchen, I realise I've left my nursing pads upstairs and milk is now drenching my nightshirt. I reach for the first thing I can find: a tea-towel hanging over the front of the oven. I put the kettle on for a cup of tea. I sit on the stool in the kitchen and, with the wind still rattling the back door, open some wedding dress magazines my best friend dropped round yesterday. Having a wedding to plan and find a date for is forcing me to look ahead to a new horizon. He didn't say it to me, because he didn't need to, but I'm certain Finn proposed now so that Mum could be at our wedding.

I know with absolute clarity that time means something different now, and what our family does with it has become the ultimate task of living.

❖ ❖ ❖

I have tried to look behind the mask of the things that terrorise me awake most and I've realised that what keeps me up most at night is not what is happening right now but Mum's death. I know nothing about what death will be like. What will death do to her? What will death do to me? What will death do to us?

I'm so scared of the answers to these questions that I still cannot even say the word out loud. The only thing I find that helps is to bring myself entirely into the present moment and be thankful for what is here, right now. This, of course, is the premise of many ancient wisdoms, but it is only now, faced with the certainty of an entirely uncertain future, that it has revealed what a life raft it is.

◆ ◆ ◆

Often, at the moment, when I'm trying to get to sleep, I lie awake polishing memories of my childhood, dusty artefacts, to try to make them vivid and clear enough to hold. I'm aware that the memories I have been reaching for most lately are those of times we spent together as a family in Scotland. The last conversation Mum and I had before she had her seizure was about what she'd like to do for her seventieth birthday.

Maybe a trip to Scotland with all the family and a group of friends? 'All I know, darling, is that if this is what 70 feels like then it's completely fabulous!' she'd said, 90 minutes before a brain tumour the size of a golf ball caused a seizure that rendered her unconscious and nearly killed her outright.

Mum and Dad both grew up in Scotland – Dad's side of the family are Scottish – and we went back at least once a year throughout my childhood. Being in Scotland awakens the cells of my childhood memories. It is a sort of spiritual home for our family, a place steeped in such deeply happy times – walking among towering, ancient mountains of verdant green, purple and slate black through dreich Scottish drizzle so dense it feels like moving through static rain; after a freezing cold swim, collecting bags of kelpie seaweed from the shores of the sea lochs for Mum's 'DIY spa' mineral seaweed baths back at our B&B; naps in the afternoon under old-fashioned eiderdowns and woollen quilts, with the endless wilderness around us.

There is a very special place on the west coast of Scotland where we are yet to go together: Plockton. A tiny fishing hamlet tucked away in the wild edges of north-west Scotland, it is one of Mum's favourite places in the world. She started going to Plockton with her girlfriends ten years ago for guaranteed decompression from the demands of her work; for long walks, to swim in the loch, to eat prawns and drink wine in the local pub till she was up dancing on the tables. We have made multiple plans in the last few years to go there together but they have been foiled by work, life and the delusion that there would always be 'next year'. Mum has often called me from the jetty in Plockton, glass of white wine in hand, after a long day walking in the prehistoric landscape of mountains and sweeping lochs, describing the most 'beautiful view she knew' that was towering around her, and talking me through everything we'd do when I went there with her.

The Isle of Skye is just across the headland from Plockton. Mum has sung Ottie 'The Skye Boat Song' since the day she was born. Hearing her sing it to her and observing it becoming generational felt like a quiet homage to the world of our family. Its melody takes me into the deep crevices of our shared love and history, to all that has always felt certain and secure. Now, though, when I too hum that timeless, lilting melody to Ottie to soothe her to sleep at bedtime, it feels like I'm sending up a prayer in a perilous storm.

I've noticed Mum talking about Scotland a lot

lately – 'Darling, we could do with a kelpie sea bath, couldn't we? Let's do a belated birthday trip when I'm feeling better.' Her frame as small as a bird.

◆ ◆ ◆

Today, Mum turns 70. It is not the birthday celebration any of us could have known it would be. Yet, here we are, not on our way to Scotland but to Matthew's house in west London, with a very small group of Mum's closest friends and our immediate family. I ring the bell and Matthew opens the door – his gentle expression, handsome face and huge heart are standing there to greet us. He opens his arms and gives me a hug that goes on longer than normal.

As I walk into the hallway filled with the rustle of helium balloons and hanging ribbons, I know what is clawing at me: the marking of time that birthdays provide doesn't feel like a counting up of years of life today, it feels like a countdown to the end. Everything about a birthday in the context of Mum's prognosis sits with such dissonance. Yes, when aligned with the lessons of 'presence' we are so lucky to be here together for her birthday at all, but is this her last birthday? Is this a day to feel pure gratitude that we are here together? Or is it OK to feel overwhelmed by the possibility that this may be her last birthday? I suppose it is all of them . . . There are so many wild and contradictory feelings. Ottie is six months old now; Mum may only have six months left.

As we drop our bags and Ottie's car seat in the hallway, the doorbell rings again. It's Mum and Dad. Matthew greets them with hugs and a very good impersonation of the celebratory spirit of birthdays. Mum disappears inside his arms. She's still in her tracksuit and looks like she's just woken up from a sleep in the car. Dad looks drawn today too. After Mum reappears from Matthew's embrace she comes to me, arms lifted, and as I wrap my arms around her, she rests her head on my shoulder.

'Darling, when is everyone arriving?' she asks. 'I'm sorry I'm not ready yet, I'm so tired today. I need to get changed but maybe I can just shut my eyes for ten minutes first?'

'Of course, Mum, that's fine. Let's go and lie down in Math's bedroom for a bit.'

So I take her arm and she leans on to me to support

her balance as we walk down the corridor into Matthew's bedroom, a cosy and quiet room at the back of the house. I walk her to sit down on the bed. I sit next to her and she immediately rests her head on my shoulder again.

'I'm tired, darling. I'm so tired.'

'I know you are, Mum, I know you are. Let's lie down for a little bit.' Her collarbones are more pronounced at the neck of her jumper today; her scalp is completely bald round the left side of her head. We curl up under the covers in Matthew's bed to the sounds of the doorbell ringing, of Annie, Luke and Eleanor arriving, of feet, more people and the rustle of more balloons and flowers ascending the stairs to the living room. She lays her head on my chest in the way I have always done to her and within moments, she's asleep. I lie looking at her outline, drawing it into my eyeballs with a black marker pen, gripping onto this feeling – of her, her body, us, together. I do not know what to do other than to love her, from my cells and my blood in a way that feels like holding on for life itself.

When Mum wakes up, I get her dressed and we go upstairs. I say hello to guests who congratulate me and

Finn on our engagement. I pose with a smile and drink my glass empty of whatever it has been filled with. I avoid eye contact. We talk but don't say what we are feeling. We clink glasses. We toast to Mum, which momentarily renders her a ghost. We eat, I push my food around my plate, we talk more, but we don't talk about 'it'. We go outside to the garden, stand in low autumn sun taking photos of her, which feels like the frantic gathering up of the remains of a fire.

Mum's friend Jonathan comes in playing 'The Skye Boat Song' on the bagpipes for her. They make a sound that could tear the sky, ancient and raw, like sorrow and solace all at once, and are so loud they will be heard throughout the small pocket of residential London streets that surround Matthew's house. Mum's friends shift their weight around on their seats, napkins rising to their eyes to pat down tears which they are trying to conceal but are impossible to stop. Mum sits with Ottie on her knees most of the afternoon. Her friend Julia gives her a hat that has 'Loved' sewn onto it in red sequins. I hope Mum is able to see this technicolour of love around her that is so vivid she could touch it.

I leave everyone in the kitchen and walk out the

front door onto the street. As I walk around the corner, I immediately start crying and sit down in the first place I can on the pavement, too drunk now to care that I am in plain sight of people walking by. I sit here until my eyes run dry and I can feel the warmth of the low sun drying the salt all over my face.

Eventually, Julia appears behind me and rests one hand on my shoulder. 'Jessie?'

Julia has long auburn hair and loving emerald eyes. As our world has contracted, she is one of the few people who has remained on the inside of our new life with us. It's funny, as the months have passed, seeing who has remained – it's not necessarily the people I had thought would be here. I don't need to say anything to Julia: my face, eyes and heart are blood red and raw for her to see.

'Oh, darling Jessie. Of course you feel like this, darling. Of course you do. Everything in the inner sanctum of your life as you knew it has changed. You have already lost so much, darling. You're grieving: what you are experiencing is anticipatory loss – you are grieving the loss of your life as it was, what you thought your future would be, the parts of Tess which are changing so quickly too. It's OK to be feeling like this, darling, it's completely normal.' She continues, 'Anyone who knows Tess can't bear to come to terms with what's happening, but everyone is aware this is most, most cruel for you.' I listen while staring into the sky, which is now 'suicidally blue', as I once heard someone describe it.

◆ ◆ ◆

I never knew it was possible to grieve *before* death had happened. Since Julia gave this monstered sadness a name at Mum's birthday lunch, I have felt the same relief and clarity I have felt when a doctor makes a diagnosis, gives a name to something that has been, until then, faceless. Anticipatory loss: I am missing her, but she is right here. I am filled with dread about everything that may come after this exact moment. I can't make plans for anything in the future because the future holds Mum's death, and I don't know who I will be or what I will be beyond it.

When I was a child, the thing I was most scared of was my mum dying. I am an adult, yet this fear is still so vicious it makes me feel miniscule and unequipped to face it. I don't feel tired but all I want to do is sleep. I don't want to talk about it because nothing, not anything or anyone, can change it. I have no comprehension of a life without her. My girlfriends, the other most important people in my world, are meeting for dinner tonight at my favourite local restaurant but I can't bring myself to see anyone.

I want Ottie to know the person I was, not the person I am now. I am scared about how this monstrous sadness is affecting her, in ways I can't yet quantify. My mum is my deepest, most unchanged sense of home. It exists within her. I am trying to recreate that experience of home, in me, for Ottie, while being hollowed myself with homesickness for a person that is still here but will soon be gone. I know in my rational mind that Mum has terminal cancer but I cannot accept it and it makes me feel pathetic and weak.

There is so much that has been lost even before death has happened.

♦ ♦ ♦

Dad brought Mum's new scans home with him from the hospital last week and they've been encased in a brown A4 envelope on the end of his desk at Lower Farm since then. He had called me his way back:

'Jessie, it's Dad.'

'Hi. What did they say?' Dreadful pause.

'Darling, listen – are you with Finn?'

'Dad, please don't do that, just tell me – what did the scan show?'

'They don't know for certain but there are three new areas towards the back of her brain that have been highlighted in the scan. They are small but they are new.'

'What? So she has three new tumours?'

'Darling – I don't KNOW!!' he said, his voice brittle, momentarily flaring. Another pause. 'They don't know for certain yet. They said these might be areas of inflammation caused by the radiotherapy and they are going to monitor her more closely for any changes. But I can tell by the look on that doctor's face again that it is not the news we were hoping for.'

This morning when I had come down to make coffee, Matthew was already in the kitchen. He told me that last night once we were all asleep, he had taken the scans out and looked at them. He said having seen the images of what may be the new tumours for himself, he had woken up with a new and unexpected feeling of acceptance about everything. So later this morning, when everyone else was downstairs in the kitchen having Dad's scrambled eggs and toast for breakfast, I took the scans out to look at them too. I knew that doing this was going to hurt, but after what Matthew had told me I felt I had to make myself do it. I held them against the Anglepoise lamp on the desk in the living room: differing shades of white and black, the winding, solid, neurological matter of her brain – with these small, white flecks at the back of her head, which are almost certainly the growth of three more tumours. The simple and biological truth of this image just brought me to tears.

However, this time, the news of the likely recurrence of Mum's tumour does feel different – unlike the first diagnosis in the summer, I'm not thrashing against it. This time I feel I am laid still, unflinching and obedient to those razors baring down. Maybe this is the feeling that Matthew had described as 'acceptance'. While I still feel so small and without any sense of true 'knowing' about any of this, I am aware that at least the silent, visceral pain of it all feels familiar now.

After breakfast, Mum, Ottie and I got back into Mum's bed again. We are spending more and more time in her bed all together. Secretly, I think that maybe death won't find her as long as we're under her duvet and I'm guarding over her like she is now, asleep to my right, Ottie asleep on the bed to my left.

Ottie's hair is thick and dark, and long enough to fill my fingertips up to my knuckles. Her cheekbones are widening like a horizon at dawn. Her eyebrows are dramatic and feathery black; her feet are stretching into the ends of the baby grows that she's now too big for, like little torpedoes.

From Mum's bed where we are, I can see out the window that the trees lining the lane outside Lower Farm are ablaze with colour. It is in death that their leaves become most vivid. Overnight, the tips of the trees have been stripped by agitating winds, so they are now only partially dressed in their bright jewel tones of ruby reds, ambers and emerald greens. Their stalks are as thin as cotton thread and most of the remaining ones are spinning, soon to release and fall to the ground. Nature destroys and recreates all at once. Ottie is now stirring on my left, and Mum turning over under the duvet on my right.

No one has ever told me the absolute truth about death. What it will do, what it will feel like, what kind of life will lie beyond it for me and for our family – not society, not music, not books, family or friends. Death is there, waiting at the end of the road for all of us, we just don't know how long that road will remain open till we come face to face with it, and how it will appear. Yet here I am. Here we are. Why is this universal experience so shrouded in secrecy?

With Mum and Ottie both so soundly asleep on either side of me, I slide myself to the end of the bed and take a photo of them. Photos of them together now are artefacts, treasures. They are how our bodies, this life together, is being accounted for.

As I'm standing at the end of the bed, Mum starts to stir. Her duvet rustles around her and her eyes blink open, till she's lying still and staring at the ceiling.

'Mum . . . you OK? Shall I get you a cup of tea?'

'Yes, darling, I'd love that.' Then she sits up and

looks straight at me – 'Are you OK, darling, are you happy?'

I smile back at her. 'Yes, Mum, I am.'

'I can't wait for Christmas and I was thinking – let's all go to Plockton for a few days after New Year's Eve? I can't think of anything I'd love more than starting the year there together. And shall we make a plan to do some wedding dress shopping together once we're back after New Year?'

'Ah, yes, I'd love that, Mum.'

There is a long pause, then she says, 'Darling, I want to do something. I need to do something for all those patients like me that I spent this summer in waiting rooms with. Will you help me?'

— *Winter 2017* —

The darkness surrounding Lower Farm is lifted with the twinkling glow of Christmas lights that are hanging from windows and Christmas trees all over the surrounding countryside. Everywhere is charged with the magic and anticipation of Christmas Eve. There is that sense that all over the world, people are returning home and usual business is slowing down to a stop.

I arrived at Lower Farm yesterday from London. Mum eagerly greeted us with her arms raised high and wide in the front doorway. Carols were on the radio in the kitchen. Dad was already busy prepping for Christmas lunch and before we even got through the door, Mum was telling us all about the presents she had bought for Ottie's first Christmas.

On the whole, I have been doing 'better' since mine and Finn's engagement. I have been seeing more of my friends; I went to a gig; I went to a best friend's birthday party. I have been enjoying the new focal points that the wedding has created, both in terms of the day-to-day distractions of looking at wedding dresses in magazines with Mum, but also the focus that the wedding has created 'out there', in that mysterious thing that I otherwise don't like to think about: The Future. Finn and I have even set a date for the wedding next summer.

But then . . . Christmas began and just the thought of planning Christmas, which may be our last together, has turned up the temperature again on some of the most vicious parts of anticipatory loss. Now, on Christmas Eve, I feel like I am in a furnace. My brain is on fire again with that sadness and hatred for what is happening, a feeling so intense that while Mum, Dad and all my siblings were downstairs wrapping presents, I came upstairs alone to my bedroom so I could scream into my pillow.

We Are Each Other

I am certain nobody noticed. As a family, we have always been good at being busy but doing nothing, but now we are keeping busy so we can avoid having to look each other dead in the eye.

I have never felt an alignment to a particular organised religion or faith, and certainly not to Christianity, but this year I am searching for any kind of spiritual consolation. So, I was pleased when Mum invited us to join her at the midnight mass service in our neighbouring village, just as she has done every other year. Dad is an atheist but Mum has always had what she describes as 'faith'. The precise definition of which she has always kept private – she has never wanted her concept of God to be questioned. But at Easter and, like tonight, for Christmas Eve, she likes to go to midnight mass.

Her younger brother, my Uncle James, died from cancer 13 years ago. After he died, for some time, Mum was wretched with a kind of sorrow I now better understand. Three months after his death, she decided to go and spend ten days in Scotland alone at a remote Benedictine Priory, where she lived in solitude and walked alone in the untouched wilderness of towering green and black mountains and pine forests. I have been learning too how the extremities of the feelings of love and sorrow create a pull to be in these sorts of spaces. The Celtic saints used to describe them as 'thin places', places where the veil between heaven and earth feels thin. Where there is that inexplicable feeling that the space between the living and the eternal has collapsed. There is a quality about these places, whether it be in an ancient ruin, or in the towering majesty of a wild natural landscape, where you can feel exquisitely alone, because you feel you could not be accompanied in the experience of being there, not even by language.

I have always placed my faith in the rational world, but now I feel 'that' world has stopped being able to offer me the reassurance and solace I need. Ultimately, I am searching for a belief system which can plausibly hold the living and the dead together, something that offers the possibility of a reunion beyond the end of life.

The concept of faith, as I understand it, is the conviction to believe in something that by its very nature cannot be proven as fact, so the act of believing is in part the act of 'faith' in itself. I think the plausible parameters of 'truth' are becoming more fluid to me too. These days, the possibility of things just being true 'enough' is a beautifully humane and gentle notion, coined by someone who understood the times when there needs to be a looser grip on fact. Because sometimes, the facts of life are just too hard to live with.

Naturally, the reasons for this new openness to the realms of faith and belief stand before me, naked: I cannot bear the thought that Mum will be dead and be completely gone from me, impossibly soon, and I need to feel a greater sense that that end point is not an end of our life together – but a continuation, of sorts.

❖ ❖ ❖

Black winter air erupts into glistening clouds in front of my, Matthew and Mum's faces as we open the car doors outside the gate to St James' Church. St James' was built in the fifteenth century – it has thick stone walls, gently sloping engraved stone and iron floors, vaulted ceilings with ornate glass and iron windows. There is that 'thin' feeling here that the Celtic saints described. During the day, you can see over the old stone wall that lines the graveyard, with its thick circle of evergreen cedar and yew trees, west across the soft, ancient, undisrupted undulations of the English countryside.

We enter and find a place near the middle of the pews. We settle in side by side, arms linked, hands and fingers clasped on the shallow wooden benches of the freezing cold carcass of the church. After a few moments, I look around to see who else is here. An older lady sitting on her own with her eyes closed, her silver white hair showing at the sides of her navy blue knitted hat. A middle-aged man with two teenage children. And then, just a few rows behind us, a man and woman, probably in their fifties. Her head rests on his shoulder and her eyes are closed, tears are silently rolling over the bridge of her nose and down her cheeks. I can recognise in her that internal feeling of wailing.

And then something occurs to me: perhaps the furnace I have been living in since the summer doesn't cut me off from humanity . . . Perhaps it connects me to it even more deeply.

I turn back around and close my eyes. I have never known so little about what the next year is going to

We Are Each Other

hold but I also know I have never been so present and awake to all that is right here in front of me, either. I squeeze my fingers into Mum's hand a little tighter; she squeezes hers into mine. Her eyes are still closed, having time with her God.

After the service, as we leave the church and step back out into the black winter air, she turns to me and says, 'I've been thinking about what I want to do, for the patients like me. I've been speaking to Dad, friends, former colleagues and they're going to help me pull together a campaign. Can we do it together, darling? Maybe we could make this whole nightmare have some purpose – make it mean something.'

◆ ◆ ◆

I push at the heavy wooden gate at the top of the hillside that is rolling down below us. Mum, Dad Matthew, Finn, Annie and I all pause to look into the view. Ottie is asleep at my chest in her sling. The rest of the family are laid up at home after Christmas lunch. Dusk is lowering into the landscape. About a mile into the view, I can see the tiny outline of our village, which is starting to glow with the twinkle of Christmas lights in every house. True to family tradition, we have driven here, to the highest Cotswold hill, to do the Christmas Day walk that we have done throughout my life. Being on this hillside all together now, it is as if the pieces of our life are being all stacked up, towering around us in plain sight.

I could walk the two-mile loop down the hill, up the pebble lane then back down through the thick pine forest to our parking place with my eyes shut. Wherever I am, I can imagine this view and how it will be changing throughout the seasons. Right now, it is its most stark and wild; the razored silhouette of the black-green pine forest towers above and around us. Sweeping down the hill are thorny hedgerows that today look like upturned seams on a jumper holding patches of faded green and browns together for as far as I can see.

A little further down the hillside below us, nestled in the taut, pale sinews of the beech trees, there is a russet brown and copper kestrel perching. Its eyes are keen and alert, wings pinned back, poised to take flight. All around us, the mossy green of the hillside meets the ashen tone of the low hanging sky. Then, out of nowhere, a beam of low winter sun finds a tear in the blanket of mute sky and the whole landscape is illuminated in iridescent pink light which holds us all as close as a prayer. I feel suddenly enveloped in an unexpected feeling of exaltation at the exquisite beauty of all that is present and before me, with Mum's left hand in my right, her fingers ice-cold at the tips and warm at her palm. No moment is wasted now.

Could it be that in this tension between life and death, we are somehow most searingly awake?

As the sky repairs itself, the pink light drains from our faces and the landscape, and my eyes regain focus down the hill again. The ground has remained frosty and hard underfoot throughout the day. As we begin the first part of the walk down the hill, arms and hands linked into one another, we start talking about our long-anticipated trip up to Plockton next week.

'Darlings, me and Dad are going to drive so we can bring all your bags with us to save you from having to bring too much luggage on the plane.'

As Mum goes on to describe the majestic beauty of the drive through the Kyle of Lochalsh which leads to Plockton, I can hear a subtle but stunning change in her speech. Suddenly, there is an irregular but frequent pause before her words – the flow of her diction is suddenly unusually bumpy. I look to my right and catch Matthew's eye; I can tell by the way his eyes dart towards mine that his stomach just flipped like mine did as she said 'd-d-d-drive'. But Mum hasn't reacted – she hasn't acknowledged it at all. She has just paused to stand still for a moment, as if just having another moment to take in the view, lifting her head a little higher, taking a deep breath in through her nose – squeezing my hand a little tighter as she does.

And then she says to us, still looking outward, 'Darlings, I'm n-n-ot afraid. When you have this kind of love in your life, what is there to possibly be afraid of?'

◆ ◆ ◆

My phone is vibrating on the kitchen counter.

'Jessie, listen, Mum has spoken to her oncologist and he's said it's not safe for her to travel for a while, so we're going to have to postpone our trip to Plockton.'

Mum takes the phone from him. 'Darling, it's M-Mum.'

'Hi Mum.'

'I'm so s-sorry, I know you'll be so disappointed, but I promise we'll go in the summer when I'm bett-tt-tt-er. When I'm bett-tt-tt-er.'

'When you're better.'

'Yes, exactly.'

◆ ◆ ◆

The first week of January in London always feels like the city is still emptied out. The light flow of traffic on the roads. The empty aisles in the supermarkets. The thin line of regulars at the bar in local pubs. The sky filling the windows tonight is so dark, so cold, that it feels as though all light has been sucked out from it completely.

Dad is in the kitchen, classical music on the radio, apron on, glass of wine in hand, cooking us a stew with greens and jacket potatoes, when Mum stands up from where she was sitting on the sofa and walks over to the kitchen table, asking us to come and sit down.

'There's s-s-something I want to talk to you about.'

I haven't heard this tone in her voice, gentle yet completely in command, since her seizure. Finn, Ottie,

Matthew, Dad and I all sit down at the table, with Mum at the head.

'Listen. I have been thinking about my c-c-c-campaign l-l-l-ong and ha-aa-rrd. I want-t-t-t — t-t-o use the position I still have, to try and make a difference — to make things for cancer patients like me better. I have been speaking to p-p-p-people, old colleagues, f-f-f-friends who re-e-e-ally know what needs to be done to change things. I c-can't t-turn away from that — and I need to do it s-s-s-oonnn. I know I h-a-a-aven't been feeling g-gg-reat but please, don't try and s-s-stop me.'

Then, mid-sentence, as she's describing all the people that want to help her, that they are going to start working on it this week, how she wants me to help her, something starts happening that I do not have a point of reference for: mid-sentence, she is trying to speak but it's as if her jaw has suddenly become disconnected from her face and she has lost the ability to move it with control or form coherent language at all.

'Euh-euhhhgg-ehhh. Euuhhhhgg.'

It sounds like a mixture of moaning and growling. Her face has completely dropped at one side, and for the first time since she was diagnosed, her eyes look wide with fear.

◆ ◆ ◆

As we walk into the oncologist's room, Mum is finishing up a phone call to her former chief advisor, who is planning her campaign launch with us. A date has been set for it in two weeks. She will give a speech, in Parliament, calling on the government for radical innovation of research, treatment and care for brain cancer patients. As we walk into the room she is distracted, but my stomach is already gripping onto itself. I hate it here. I fucking hate it with all I am. Her oncologist comes in and Mum says goodbye on the phone.

The oncologist sits down then opens her file as if it were a business meeting. After the collapse in her speech a few days ago, Mum was put on a very high dose of steroids to help 'control her symptoms', which for now has done some immediate work on restoring an ability to form sentences. He holds the scan up to the lightbox and, as he starts to talk, I feel leaden and mute.

He begins, 'This scan confirms that the three

new areas we identified at the last scan were not inflammation, but are in fact three, now substantial-sized tumours at the back of your brain, Tessa, each approximately the size of a 10p piece. But this here' – he points to the middle of her brain – 'this white cloud here is also cancer. But it looks like mist because this cancer is diffused. The cancer is now profoundly established in the centre of your brain too, Tessa. Do you understand what this means? I recommend we think about a "salvage strategy" of chemotherapy,' he says. 'As you know, we have no other treatment to offer you, but because of the rate of the progression the scans have shown, I am recommending this time we give you a higher dose. Because of the high dose, we will have to monitor you very closely on it, but it's either that or . . . Or we do nothing at all, and . . . And we will have to start talking about palliative care.'

As we leave the consultation room she immediately starts talking. 'D-d-d- d-don't even sa-sa-say it to me. Don't say it. I am d-doing it and nothing is g-g- going to stop me.' She says she has already agreed that one of her best friends and former colleagues, George, is going to sit next to her in the House of Lords while she delivers her campaign speech. 'If I can't s-s-s-peak, if I c-c-c-an't get through it, George will finish it for me.'

❖ ❖ ❖

The day has not yet broken into itself at the window; the sky is a dense mahogany blanket. Mum's flat is already bustling with the very particular hum of activity that our house was so often filled with when I was growing up. Her former life, that she has been severed from for so long, has been mainlined back into her kitchen – Dad is handing out rounds of coffees and croissants to Mum's former chief advisors, press team and former private secretary, who are all reunited here to brief, advise and cheer Mum on as she prepares for a morning of pre-recorded radio interviews that she will do from her kitchen to launch her campaign.

I finish doing Mum's makeup – soft brown in her eyebrows, dark grey eyeliner and mascara that makes her eyes ignite like pale blue sapphires. Then I walk back into the kitchen and stand next to her beloved, long-standing former advisor Peter, as Mum begins checking her microphone clipped onto her shirt, sitting facing the journalist who has come to the house to do an exclusive interview with her for Radio 4. As she leans into the first questions, her eyes are alert with her characteristic warmth and focus.

Just before she begins, Peter leans in with a smile rising in his eyes that looks almost like relief – 'There she is, the Queen back on her throne.'

Many of the people in this room have been visitors over these past months, but no one knows how close to the precipice she really is. Her speech today is sharper, more fluent than it has been in weeks, which is being remarked on as 'miraculous' by the few standing close to me in the room. But I know that the reason is more specific than that – it is because of what I just found in her bathroom before I came upstairs. I was going to get her morning medications ready to take to her, and when I went to get her steroids I could see that the bottle, which was full last night, is now almost empty. She found a rare moment of privacy last night before bed and took more than a week's dose at once.

◆ ◆ ◆

The floor of the House of Lords is packed on every bench. The gallery we occupy alongside friends and other family is so full that most people are standing. The whole room hushes to a quiet as the speaker announces her and Mum gets to her feet. George is sat to her right as her fallback with her manuscript in his hands too. She begins — her frayed remaining threads of speech have been twisted by steroids into fragile ropes to carry her from one word to the next — but it is her sheer grit and determination that holds her steady through every word, almost without falter. She arrives at her closing words:

In the words of Seamus Heaney — I am not afraid. I am just afraid that this very important new approach will be put in the 'too difficult' box.

Now I just ask the government, doctors, patients and the health system to work together... In the end, what gives a life meaning is not only how it is lived, but how it draws to a close. I hope that this debate will give hope to other cancer patients like me so that we can all live well with cancer, not just be dying of it — all of us — for longer.

Jess Mills

The whole floor of the House of Lords and the packed gallery rise to their feet for the first standing ovation in the history of the upper house, that goes on for so long it feels like it may never end.

Under the long shadows of her approaching death, she is teaching us all what it means to truly live.

— *Spring 2018* —

'H-h-haaappyyy bbb-bbb-bbbirthday to y-y-ou, h-haaappyyy bbb-bbb-bbbirth – d-ddd day to you, h-haaappyyy bbb-bbb-bbbirthday, dear Ottsie – h-haaappyyy bbb-bbb-bbbirthday . . . ' – silence – 't–t-t-t-too y-y-yyouuu!'

I can't see Mum's face on the video call because Ottie is holding my phone, on the screen of which Mum's blue eyes and wide open singing mouth and teeth are moving in and out of focus, filling the whole screen and making Ottie erupt in elated chants of 'Mamamamama', 'Ganny, Ganny Ganny.'

Mum starts trying to speak again. 'D-d-d-ch-che-ssa-saa.'

Dad takes the phone. 'Hi, darling, happy birthday to Otts. Mum is saying we're on our way to the hospital to pick up her steroids and then we'll come over for birthday tea. Not sure what time we'll get to you, with waiting times, but will be there soon as we can. Gosh, imagine Otts being one already!'

On the rare days we are not together now, we talk to Mum on the phone, mostly on video. It's easier to read what she is saying, or trying to say, from the visual cues of her expression, the look of confusion in her eyes which lets me know she's about to stammer on her words.

The focus of the conversations has become very narrow and repetitive; mainly we just bumble through talking about, or to, Ottie together. Ottie is the thing, the person, the subject she finds easiest to communicate about now. I think this is because all she needs to do is express love to her, which even with the most distressing and rapid recent deterioration in her language, she can still do in a very distilled way, with her characteristic ebullience. The only word she doesn't stumble on now is 'love'. So, often, that is what she just says to Ottie on repeat: 'Love, love, love, love, love, love, love, love.'

I'm still holding the phone with the video call on – we are not speaking now, just being together. I can hear the sounds of the inside of the car in the background – the click of Dad indicating, the windscreen wipers going back and forth – as I'm looking at Ottie, now halfway across the room from me, with an unusual moment of distance and perspective. I don't think I will ever be able to make sense of this division of myself – how the width of her shoulders, the span of her ribcage and those kicking limbs that emerged from my body a year ago have grown into the determined shoulders of a little toddler, strong arms outstretched, holding onto her wooden trolley; dramatic, feathery black eyes glistening with the thrill of feeling her legs and feet beneath her, now strong enough to walk a few elated steps across the living room of our flat and into my arms.

There is something about motherhood which still feels like disbelief – maybe that never changes. I think about how I'd love to ask Mum if she felt the same way about me, or if she still does. But her eyes are looking confused again, her mouth is stuck on the word 'love, love, love, love, love'.

With the phone still in my hand, Ottie is sucking Mum's face again on the screen and I can see through the glass of our garden door and a sudden downpour of bitterly cold wet sleet that the beginning of spring's annual offering of new life is pushing up against the freezing black earth. The days at the moment are still brief and pale, but robust shoots of silvery green and pristine white snowdrops are starting to poke their way through the soil of the garden like little torpedoes.

As Ottie is expanding, growing into life, Mum is shrinking, contracting with the forward and irreversible motion of something else . . . something which is changing the quality of her skin so sometimes she looks translucent. Every so often, she holds her hand up to Dad's face, as if she's remembered something urgent, and then turns and says to me, as an instruction: 'Love D-dad.'

The cycle of life is spinning so vividly between us today I could reach out and trace it with my fingertips.

◆ ◆ ◆

We Are Each Other

I run from the shower not quite quickly enough to answer my phone, so I find a voicemail instead from my brother Matthew.

'Hey Jess . . . You OK? Give me a call back when you can. Listen, I've just been speaking to Dad, we've had an idea I wanted to talk to you about. We were thinking, maybe you and Finn should bring the wedding forward, and do it soon, like . . . really soon?' Pause. He doesn't need to say why. 'If you want to do it we'll all rally — we'll make sure everything is ready in time. Sorry, I know this is a lot to think about but . . . have a chat with Finn and call me back? Love you.'

❖ ❖ ❖

I wake up in bed next to my life-long best friends, Mond and Bella. Heavy velvet curtains frame the thick, dark wood of the four-poster bed, which has a bath at the end of it. We drink champagne in bed for breakfast. Mond paints my nails, Bella plays music probably too loudly for a smart hotel at this time of the morning on our speaker. We chat, cry and laugh as I have my hair and makeup done by two other childhood friends, who arrive at 9am with their characteristic and irresistible flair for fun and mischief. My seven bridesmaids arrive and we drink more champagne and dance around the room till Mum and Dad arrive, and then we all pile into a stream of black taxis to drive to the wedding venue.

We arrive at Clissold House, in the middle of Clissold Park in Hackney, under a bright blue early spring sky filled with racing white clouds. My bridesmaids go ahead and I wait at the doors of the room with Mum and Dad. I can hear the low hum of chatter and the playlist Finn has made for the ceremony, which takes me back to the time he and I fell in love.

Mum and Dad walk me down the aisle and as I find Finn's eyes, seeing him surrounded by our best friends, family, Nicolette with Ottie on her knees, it brings on a feeling of utterly delirious love for him and everyone in this room, so all I can do as I walk towards him is laugh, tears streaming from my eyes. As I stand to face him, I can feel my hands start to tremble. We are pronounced husband and wife and the room erupts in cheers so loud they rattle the window panes.

We Are Each Other

We walk out of the registry office to Jonathan playing the bagpipes. As we process out, Mum spontaneously erupts into dance and everyone spins each other around the entrance hall to the ancient wailing, euphoric sound of the bagpipes, that is so loud and so raw it could crack the sky open. We all pack into taxis and head to my favourite Italian restaurant on one of London's perfectly cobbled backstreets behind Columbia Road, and drink negronis and eat pasta and seafood and tiramisu.

After pudding, Mum spontaneously climbs up onto her chair and gives a speech to the restaurant packed with our whole world. It is mainly sounds, not words, but everyone understands what she is saying. At the end, in a sudden slipstream of coherence, she just keeps repeating at the top of her voice, 'There is so m-m-m-much more to do . . .! There is s-so m-much more to do . . .! There is so much more to do!' Everyone cheers and raises their arms and hands clapping at the ceiling. The room is full of eyes that are sparkling at the life-affirming courage and beauty of her.

In the long shadows of approaching death, we are being charged to live from our cells and our bones as if every moment is our last. There is a technicolour of beauty and sorrow, joy and presence between everyone that is even more vivid for all to see and feel because of the darkness that surrounds it. I am pulled in, hugged, kissed on my face by every person I love most in the world. Then we leave the restaurant. Nicolette gathers up Ottie's things to take her home for bedtime, and the sight of Ottie in her arms driving away in a taxi makes my heart almost burst with the love and gratitude I feel for both of them.

Then we walk to our favourite local pub up the road and dance on the tables with our best friends till a new day starts to make the night sky glow pale blue at the windows. Finn and I leave the last remaining friends in a black cab and drive back to the hotel through London as it's waking up. Then we drink more champagne in the bath together as the morning service begins to rattle through the corridors of the hotel around us. Then we climb into bed, and then inside each other's bodies, until we collapse into sleep.

I remember who I still am, I remember who I can still be. I remember all the beauty and love that life can hold, even when death is waiting at the door.

We Are Each Other

❖ ❖ ❖

I am searching everywhere, in literature, in music, in films, for something that can mirror back to me this entirely ordinary experience of the preparation for the death of a mother. Yet I can find nothing of significance. I know that the death of a person of her age, who has lived the extraordinary life she has lived, could not be considered a tragedy. I know it is the wish of every parent that they would die before their child. I know it is right that she should go before me. I know I am so lucky to have lived inside her love until I am an adult and a mother myself. Yet the prospect of her being dead and being gone from my life, my daughter's life, my family's life, makes me feel like I am preparing for a death of everything – because there is no place in my life that my love for her, and hers for me, doesn't touch. It is the longest love I have known. It is what I am made from. I cannot bear to imagine this life, in which she is dead and gone from me.

❖ ❖ ❖

The air is warm, again. Cherry blossom has erupted in raspberry-ripple explosions covering whole trees lining the lane outside Lower Farm. I'm getting Ottie ready for her bath and the windows are ajar, inviting flutters of warm breeze over my arms and neck. Late afternoon sun is cast across the bathroom wall, looking as pure as honesty. The floor is littered with Ottie's bath toys, discarded clothes and tiny shoes with mud on their soles from the day in the garden.

Inside my head, the war I am fighting against Mum's death is everywhere. Deep, wide, black and purple bruises have been appearing all over her for the past few days, so first thing this morning Dad took her to the hospital to have her bloods tested.

As I lift and lower Ottie into the bath, she stomps her feet in shrieks of delight, the water splashing up around her. The phone starts ringing in my pocket. It's Dad, he's with Mum and her oncologist.

'Hi Dad.'

'Hi, darling. Can you talk?'

'I've just got Ottie in the bath, but yes. Have you got the results?'

'Darling, I'm here with the doctor – I thought it

might be helpful for you to talk to him, so I'm going to put the phone on the loudspeaker, OK?'

'OK.'

Ottie is now clapping her hands on the small mountains of bubbles building round the running water. She is still shrieking as he starts talking so I have to clamp the phone firmly to my ear.

'Hello, Jess. Tessa's results are showing a very low platelet count, caused by the chemotherapy. Platelets are what enable the blood to clot and when they are very low, the blood cannot clot anymore, which can cause internal bleeding, which is what the bruising on Tessa is caused by. Jess, I've just told your mum and dad, and I imagine you are already aware of this too – but I can also see today a very significant decline in Tessa's clinical state – specifically in her speech and overall cognition.' Then, one of those monstrous pauses. 'Because of both these things, Tessa cannot continue to take the chemotherapy. Which means, as of now, she is not going to be having any more active treatment. Do you understand what this means? Jess, it means there is nothing more that can be done for her. It means it's time to be brave.'

My eyes are focusing on that same place on the bathroom wall again, which is still cast in that honest sunlight. Ottie is still clapping at the bubbles with delight as they erupt in the air in front of her eyes. As I fully register these words and the new and certain facts they contain, the fight that has been living in the muscles in places inside me that are so deep they have no name starts to soften and release, like the fingers of an opening palm.

There is nothing that I or anyone else can do to rescue her from it now. There is nothing that I or anyone else can do to stop it. All there is left to do is to stand at the windows, watching on in obedient horror as the most sacrosanct components of her, those that are so intricate and unique in their complexity, wisdom and brilliance, are held to the fire until they catch, and burn.

My task has never been so plain: wait. Love her from my cells while it burns her entirely.

I'm still holding the phone to my ear, though neither I nor the doctor are speaking anymore. Something suddenly comes to me, delivered as absolute Truth, the kind of distilled Truth that possibly only death can reveal.

We Are Each Other

That from this moment now, until death comes, she is, and we are, free.

❖ ❖ ❖

As death waits at the door, the world has become the size of Mum's bed.

An hour ago, Mum and Ottie fell asleep just after they had both picked at the scrambled eggs on toast that Dad had brought up on a tray for Mum's breakfast. Dad also put a small posy of pale yellow primroses on the tray for her today. They have started appearing in corners of the garden in the last few days.

I have been lying here behind her now for over an hour, my arms around her soft stomach, my face nestled into the back of her neck and head, which is covered with soft silver prickles of new hair growth – the innocence of renewal. Ottie is stretched out asleep behind me on her back. Today, I've pulled the duvet up a bit higher around all our faces, so we're almost entirely hidden. I still secretly have this feeling that as long as we stay in this bed, and as long as I hold onto Mum just like this, then death will not be able to find her and take her from us, so I'm trying to make sure we are all here together, like this, as much as possible, just in case.

As I am staring at the posy of primroses, thinking about other ways we could hide Mum from death, she starts to stir and sits up on her side. Still with her eyes closed, she gestures for a drink of water, which I shuffle up the bed to reach for, then hold to her lips. As she's propped up, I move around Ottie to run Mum her morning bath, which each day now we fill to the brim with all her favourite tinctures and oils.

Outside the bathroom window, the late morning sky is a show of colours that contain the ashen tones of something that is disappearing. Mum opens her sky-blue eyes and as they find mine, they lift into a smile in the way they do when she says 'I love you'. I kiss her on the cheek, then put my arms round her to steady her at her elbows and walk her to her bathroom. With her eyes now closed, she lifts her arms above her head like a child so I can lift her white and blue striped nightdress off, revealing soft, warm flesh that bears the indiscriminate brutality of a battlefield. My stomach clenches: huge black and purple bruises are spread deep and wide all over the tops of her arms, her ribs and thighs. She stands, not moving. Her eyes are now open again and she is staring blankly at the wall. Then she turns to me and says something I haven't heard her say in this way since childhood: 'Ba-ba-bb-ba, d-da?' And we mirror a smile because I know exactly what she means. She means for me, her and Ottie to get in the bath together.

So I undress my mum and my daughter, the cornerstones of my being, and then myself, so we are each our animal bodies of soft flesh, bone and hair. Then I hold Mum's arms at her elbows to steady her as she climbs in and descends into the warm lavender water and bubbles that rise and crackle around her stomach. Ottie and I climb in with her. We lay submerged, momentarily freed from diminishing time, in a place where love feels bigger than death.

❖ ❖ ❖

Incredibly, Mum is still able to take her favourite walk each day: 15 minutes down the single-track lane that runs outside Lower Farm to the oak tree that marks the halfway mark between our village and the next. Most days we go while Dad is cooking, and Finn, Matthew and I walk on either side of Mum, with Ottie's small and eager little hand in my other hand as she makes tiny, joyful steps with us through the dappled, lacey green lanes, under the sparkling blue spring skies. We walk together as one appendage.

Mum feels so light today, like a puppet, and although it is warm, her hands feel cold. She doesn't have her hat on and new tufts of soft and downy silver hair are glowing in the sun. As we turn the corner to the expanse of view to our left, I look up and it is as though she has been drawn into my vision with sunlight. Then, with a sudden clarity in her speech, the kind of which she hasn't had for weeks, she starts speaking, still looking straight ahead:

'Darlings, I'm v-very tired, but I'm very h-happy. And I just f-f-feel that, th-th-th-this thing of us being together, it just g-g-g-goes on forever. We are each other.' She continues walking, looking ahead, her hand and fingers squeezing into mine tighter. Her expression is pure serenity.

We have not spoken about her death together since that time in the restaurant before her surgery last summer. It has been a black sun between us, something that is too dark to look at, too unthinkable to name. But in this moment, which is the first time I have felt her lean towards talking about it with us, I am struck, mostly, that this doesn't feel like a conversation about death at all. It feels like a conversation about love.

❖ ❖ ❖

Everywhere, the earth has exploded into a symphony of spring colour it sings by heart. A year ago, on this exact day, Ottie was nine weeks old. It was my birthday, the beginning of one of those unremarkably perfect days that has become hyper-illuminated in my memory against the backdrop of the new, dark world that was silently approaching. Throughout my life, birthdays have always been packaged up and delivered by Mum in reliable form, and this day was true to our traditions: an afternoon was cleared in our diaries and a favourite lunch spot in Soho was booked, where we 'gassed' our way through clattering plates of things to share, accompanied by glasses of birthday fizz 'just for you' that Mum drank most of. Then we linked arms and continued 'gassing' our way through Soho's perfect London streets, which in early May were humming with early summer pink tickets for lunchtime boozing. Every time I walk through Soho on a day like this, I feel ignited in my lifelong love for its old cobbled backstreets pulsating with an irresistible allure of the forbidden at every corner, even at 2pm. Walking along them on this day with Ottie between us, I was hit with a heady potion of presence and nostalgia that cast a rose-gold glow over everything.

As a young woman, Mum made most of her own clothes before she could afford to buy them. A bit of retail therapy, therefore, has never lost its novelty, so she had a light skip in her step as we walked up Carnaby Street after lunch. One moment in these few hours is stored at the top of my memory. An ill-judged and sweat-inducing first attempt to dress my postpartum body in clothes two sizes too small had just been remedied by Mum whipping round to skilfully select some clothes to rescue my plummeting spirits. I pulled back the dressing room curtain to get Mum's take on a promising black silk dress to a reveal a snapshot of the magic of our ordinary life: Ottie curled into Mum's neck while she gently sang to her, with a lifetime of these birthday days together ahead of us.

We Are Each Other

That day was 19 days before her seizure, the last halcyon day documented in photos. We were smiling into blue skies so bright we couldn't see the assassin lurking in plain sight. When I look at photos of this day now, I see how our lives are held together by the paper-thin skin of chaos, how the scalpel was already poised to make precise, life-tearing incisions. I had thought the 'changing room moment' was showing the future to me, but it was a reflection on the surface of a bubble so fragile it was burst by the stillness of the air holding it. How audacious, to be this happy. To be ignited so fully by a benevolent order of things, to believe in the pageant of our lives.

Exactly one year later, birthday form is being upheld in a suffocatingly firm embrace. I've spent the last 11 and a half months rejecting what's happening so quantumly that I believed it could be manifest. But now, I want to throw myself against the wall of my terror until I can peer through the cracks to see what is beyond it. With Ottie on my hip, I take slow, sinking steps across the spongy, striped lawn. The spring air is still, filled with the ambient sounds of glass on glass as wine and beers are poured by my brothers and sisters, who have all just arrived with my nieces and are congregated in the garden, with their best efforts to make it a happy day. The fragile pretence of normality is being performed with love and precision.

I have learned how to display the mechanical etiquette of 'normal' social interaction very well by now. The muscles of my face lift and draw back to create that smile from my mouth that parts like a cut. I keep eye contact when my thoughts are contorting. I tread the line of small talk within palatable boundaries. But today, the grip around my heart is so tight, I can't move my body or face around it.

After our 'hellos', we walk through the back door of the kitchen into the busyness of birthday lunch being prepared. Dad is in his apron, agitating. Not able to produce a smile, his eyebrows raise in acknowledgement of us.

'Jessie. Now, Mum is still lying down upstairs, she's suddenly got a terrible headache. I just checked on her and she's still snoozing, so if you don't mind, I think we should let her stay asleep for as long as she needs to – even if that means she doesn't come down for your lunch.'

'Sure, Dad,' I say. 'I'll just go and get changed upstairs.'

I walk through the strange normality of the hallway and start slow, heavy steps upstairs. The woollen carpet is hot underfoot. As I reach the top of the stairs, I can see that the door to Mum's bedroom is ajar. I walk towards it and pause. Then, with the push of a disobedient child, it swings open. The curtains are pinned back wide and the room is floodlit in sunshine. As I find my position at the side of her bed, a soft breeze feathers the skin of my bare arms and neck.

For a few minutes, with deadened eyes and a clenched heart, I stay standing. Observing our separateness. Observing her sleep.

Everything she does now embodies the courage of surrender. Even when she sleeps, she sleeps courageously. I perch on the edge of the bed, rustling the pristine white cotton sheets encasing her meringue duvet with the weight of my body, leaning in to feel the warmth of her skin. Above the low chatter of my family congregating in the garden below, the wood pigeon in the silver birch tree sends out its throaty call, which sounds like a mourning song.

I move in closer, needing the embrace of her soft stomach and arms to hug away a nightmare. While still encased in sleep, she turns in her burrow towards me and her arms open to hold me like only she can, with love huge and certain between us. Nothing more to be said. Just our hearts beating at the walls of our bodies, her arms squeezing acknowledgement around me.

The increasing disorientation she has been masterful at concealing is now entirely in the room with us. She searches with her tongue on the roof of her mouth for language. I sit up on my side to take her in. Her crystal blue eyes are foggy with rest, and with something else – a ribbon of smoke through a page of blank sky. Her brain is being incinerated on the insides. She has new, marbled, purple marks on the skin around her temples. I am sure she is bruising now even from our hugs and kisses.

'It's all for you, darling,' she had said to me when she started the double dose of futile chemo those weeks ago, handing over her body to us in our war against her death.

I sit her up in her bed and pass her a glass of water in silence. I want to grip this moment and wrestle it still, until my nails draw blood. There is no place for words anymore. None will do, other than those she says now, which she speaks with her palm pressed at my heart: 'I l-love you f-f-forever.'

No moment has existed like this moment now. My voice raises just above a choke. 'I love you forever too, Mum.'

For the first time, these words hang steady and portent between us. All the muscles of my heart are cradling a pounding certainty: this is the beginning of our unimaginable goodbye.

'Jess! Tess!' Luke's bellowing baritone voice sounds up the stairs. 'Lunch is on the table.' I spray a spritz of lavender on both of our faces and I set to the normal routine of helping her out of bed, slipping on her slippers and steadying her one step at a time down the stairs. The most amiable patient, responsive to the gentlest touch of persuasion.

We walk into the kitchen to find Dad in a sweat serving things out onto dishes, but as Mum and I walk in, he looks up and pauses. An involuntary smile rises out of his expression, as if he is seeing her for the first time walking down the aisle to marry him.

'Hello, my perfect darling. Matthew, will you carry the plates out so I can take Mum?'

There is something entirely different among us today. Mum is changing matter in front of our eyes; she is becoming the translucent quality of twilight.

It's clear from the line of wine and beer bottles already empty by the bin that booze has been flowing as medicine to soften the edges on everything today. As Mum and Dad walk arm in arm out of the kitchen, my sister Annie is on her way in to retrieve another bottle of wine from the fridge. And as I stand between the fridge and the garden door, the words I have refused to let myself formulate in my brain or my mouth speak themselves:

'Annie. Mum's dying.'

'Oh, my darling – come here.' She holds me tight to her as waters roar through us, bursting the banks that have contained them. With my face buried in the wet curve of her neck, her arms still tight around me, I raise my gaze to meet the stare of death entirely. And as I hold it, I feel an entirely unexpected feeling of peace and complete surrender.

One of the benefits of having a big, bustling family

We Are Each Other

is that it's easy to hide a red blotchy face among the clattering of dishes and small grandchildren clambering onto their seats. I find my seat at the table next to Mum. We clasp each other's hands and don't let go. The air feels different on my skin; could this thing called surrender already be revealing a magnitude of mercy, of peace?

After lunch, the paddling pool is filled, its refracting blue light dancing on the walls of the garden while my nieces' little naked bodies, sticky with too many helpings of Dad's homemade chocolate ice cream, skid with delighted squeals in and out of the water sprinkler. Mum, Ottie and I bask in the cool shade on her sun lounger under the silver birch tree. The heads of her coral pink peonies are hung heavy, ready to bloom. There is no other world beyond the walls of the garden now.

◆ ◆ ◆

Night has just risen around Lower Farm – the curtains are not yet drawn, so the sky is glistening black at the windows. The thorny stems, tiny leaves and tight new buds of the rose bush by the window are now cast in pale shadows of moonlight along the windowsill. Mum has been asleep next to me since lunchtime.

Her face is now in darkness, pressing deep into her pillow. She is so much more than skin can hold, but apparently we will not be able to hold on to any of her when she goes. Flickering like a flame, so nearly gone. Stay. Stay. Stay.

◆ ◆ ◆

Mum can only say two words now.

Everything, whittled down to this, which she says with eyes as wide as moonlight: 'Love, Forever.'

◆ ◆ ◆

I promised Mum I'd go to London yesterday. Her campaign has galvanised the national community of brain cancer charities, patient groups, scientists and frontline NHS staff, who are all committed to work together to deliver her vision to improve research, treatment, care and survival outcomes for patients like her. The campaign will be called the Tessa Jowell Brain Cancer Mission.

'Sso-ssss-sss-ch-cch — Ppp,' she said, lifting her

hands to my cheeks as I left the house to catch the train to meet them all at the Department of Health on Victoria Street for the afternoon to discuss how we are going to begin the work. I knew from the expression in her eyes that she was telling me she was proud of me.

As I left, I felt a feeling that I have heard her describe to me so many times growing up – that feeling of the fire of purpose, the possibility of change, being lit in the solar plexus. Though, entering the Department of Health, I felt like an imposter in this forum, as I introduced myself to the charity CEOs, the neurosurgeons, scientists, senior NHS representatives and members of the government – until I saw the faces of the other patients and their family members, including the father of the young man Mum had observed in the waiting room last summer, but today without his son. I recognised him from the hospital but we had never been properly introduced till now. He told me that Sam had died five weeks ago, two days after his nineteenth birthday. I felt overcome with emotion at the candour and courage of this statement, and then watched as the shock and agony of his new reality flooded his eyes. Neither of us could speak anymore – so I stepped towards him and we hugged. Then I told him Mum has lost nearly all her ability to speak and is sleeping pretty much all the time now. He told me Sam slept all the time at 'the end' too. *'The End'*. I still cannot comprehend it.

I know today, with an unexpected feeling of comfort, that working with this extraordinary group of people to deliver Mum's campaign when she is not here physically could create a way in which I can imagine her still implied in the future – a future in which I will be doing more for her than just burying her.

❖ ❖ ❖

I stayed in London overnight and I am now at Paddington, waiting to get the 7am train back to Lower Farm. The back of my nose and throat is peppered by the thick, grey diesel fumes that are being churned into the vaulted glass ceilings of the station. As I climb the steps into my carriage, that distinctive smell of train seats and buffet coffee replaces the diesel fumes.

My eyes are hot and tight, gripped at the back of their sockets by a night of haunting, anxious sleep. As I turned off the light and slid under my duvet last night, I felt as if a large metal hook had been inserted into my stomach, and it was pulling at me to get back to Mum at Lower Farm. I lay there feeling butchered by my separation from her, unable to sleep for hours and wishing I had driven to London so I could have just left in the middle of the night.

Now, as the train leaves the station, I look out the window at the pale blue and yellow sky covering the hum of the city rising up to meet another normal day. As the train reaches its full speed, the city starts to blur past the window until it opens out onto the landscape of the lower spine of England – a patchwork of glistening fields in shades of verdant lime greens and acid yellows. I feel now, with absolute clarity, how the ultimate 'truth' of death is silently covering over everything and everyone – over me, over the teenage boy sitting across from me at the table seat, over the conductor announcing our next stop. The finite, mortal nature of absolutely everyone and everything seems to intensify the purity of the sunshine, the blue of the sky, the movement of the oak trees lining the fields blurring past the window, and it makes my skin suddenly ignite into goosebumps in wonder and awe for all that is here and still so, so alive.

As I step off the train and walk to the taxi rank, my back pocket vibrates against my tailbone. Dad's name is flashing on the phone screen which triggers a spike of adrenaline, so that by the time the phone is lifted to my ear, my chest and ears are pounding like a red orb and I have to push the phone closer to my ear to hear him.

He doesn't say hello.

He just starts speaking.

As he does, I realise I haven't ever imagined what his voice would sound like when he said these words, that it would rise and fall like this, in between long pauses and ocean-sized breaths:

'Sweetheart. I went down to make Mum her tea and breakfast this morning while she was still asleep and came back to give it to her . . .

'But I couldn't wake her.

'Darling.

'The palliative care nurses are here already and they say Mum has had a big bleed in her brain overnight.

'She's so peaceful.'

Oh god.

'Where are you? The nurse says we have a day, maybe two.'

Every moment that has come before now has been preparation for this moment.

Within minutes, I'm in a taxi speeding towards Lower Farm. I call Dad again. 'Can I speak to her . . . ?'

'Yes, darling – she can hear you.'

'Mum . . . Mumma . . .

'I'm coming. I'm coming, Mum.

'I love you forever.

'Please wait for me.'

As the taxi winds through the lanes that lead to Lower Farm, my eyes are closed. I call Finn. He's already left Lower Farm with Ottie and is taking her to stay with friends who live nearby. Nicolette is on her way from Shimpling to be with them.

'Don't worry about us,' he said. 'Just be with her for as long as it takes.

'We love you.'

As he hangs up the phone, sunlight is strobing in my eyelids but I know exactly where I am. Every bend and bump tells me that I am nearly there. I open the taxi door with the lane still moving beneath me. I'm running though I can't feel my legs, through the back door and up the stairs onto the landing outside the bedroom, where my dad is waiting, already talking to me.

'We had a perfect day yesterday. We went for pizza, she had a cocktail. She was so sleepy but she was so happy. We walked to the tree and the sun was shining. She walked the whole way holding my arm. And then we got to the tree, and she turned and held my face, and she kissed me. Oh god. I didn't know she was saying goodbye. The sun was shining on her face and she was perfect. Oh god, my darling. My perfect darling. She was so tired, so I lay with her while she slept.'

They say only the dying can tell you how long they have left. *Then she held my face and she kissed me.*

The palliative care team are assembled on the landing between Mum and Dad's bedroom and the study, and one of the nurses steps towards me and catches my arm, rerouting me away from the bedroom.

'Jessie, hello, I'm Sarah. I just wanted to speak to you before you go in to see your mum. I'm a palliative care nurse and me and my colleague Pam are going to be with you and your mum for as long as you need us.'

'Is Mum dying?'

'Yes, my love. Your mum is dying. Your dad called

us when he couldn't wake her this morning, and the palliative care consultant has assessed her and she confirmed she has had what we call a huge "cerebral event", which means she has had a large brain haemorrhage. She is not entirely unconscious but is very, very deeply asleep. We have already given her some morphine and an anti-anxiety medication and will be able to keep her comfortable and make sure she is in no pain or distress for as long as it takes. Jessie, we are here to make sure she will be in no pain and she will be in no distress – do you understand? That means all you need to do now is to be with Mum. I saw her trying to open her eyes when your dad put you on loudspeaker just now. She's waiting for you – she will know that you are here.'

I walk three steps across the landing to the doorway of her bedroom. The windows are open. Bright morning sunshine is hitting her bed. New buds of her climbing roses have opened into pale yellow flowers and are tapping at the window frame. Yesterday's cowslips are still fresh in the vase next to the bed. Her lavender spray is next to her glasses. All the furniture in the room has been rearranged. Mum and Dad's double bed has been pulled out into the middle of the room like an island and she is in the middle of it on her side – not in a position that she would ever normally lie in, propped up by her pillows on top of her meringue duvet. She's wearing the pyjamas that she had joked about not liking anymore because they weren't her colours. I can see the profile of her face, the silver halo of her hair, her feet, her toes, the curve of her knees and the porcelain skin of her shoulders. Her eyes are closed so deeply they are turning inwards. Her contours, skin textures, bones and areas of softness of flesh on her body that I know in their detail look exactly the same, yet she is dying. Death is no longer hidden in the shadows. Death is here now, happening for all to see in the bed I thought could hide her, under this perfectly ordinary spring sky.

I kick off my shoes, climb on top of the bed and wrap my arms around her like a cape. I lie still behind her for a moment because my heart feels clenched and is beating tight and hard, my brain throbbing like a heartbeat on the inside of my skull. I don't feel scared. I feel too miniscule and insignificant to feel fear. Death has rendered me a speck on the surface of the universe.

We Are Each Other

She is, I am, we are at the mercy of something more powerful than anyone or anything else. The absolute presence of each moment is being inserted into my brain like a fishhook through my eye socket as we lay together, rooted to each other, still unable to believe that death will split us apart.

Could it be that death, like birth, is the ultimate lesson in what is bearable?

I cradle her body that is hotter than I have ever felt a human body, filled with a strange heat of dying. I find her hands and hold them into her stomach. I feel her squeeze mine back.

'There's nothing you need to say, Mum. Nothing unsaid. Nothing you need to do. I love you forever. I love you forever.'

Then the grip of her hand and fingers starts to release and I know that I have never observed courage comparable to this perfectly still, silent preparation to surrender to death. Dying isn't making her small, it is making her as magnificent and as valiant as a goddess of the sky. I am not speaking to her with my voice anymore. I have moved my voice to my heart, where I know she hears me.

Jess Mills

I didn't know death could be like this. How quiet it could be: the sound of her breathing, the occasional rustle of the duvet, now the small patter of rain at the window. Dad is bringing me and the nurses biscuits and cups of tea that are left till they are cold – even in death, our roles remain unchanged.

I can hear the intermittent voices of the nurses in the hallway talking about drug dosages. Their conversation sounds cool and ordinary, like a teacher making ticks on a school register. Matthew arrives breathless, hands shaking, just after she has been heavily dosed on more morphine and anti-anxiety meds, but the sound of his voice makes her momentarily try to open her eyes – eyelids alone lifting a lead blanket. Matthew and I sit together in silence, holding her hands and holding each other, while her clothes from yesterday, filled with the smell of her alive, lie around us like wilted lilies. After a while, Matthew asks if he can have some time with her alone, so I leave them and go to find Sarah.

I want to know: what is going to happen? How is she going to die?

'Jess, just as the body knows how to grow into life and how to give birth, it knows how to die. Death of course can happen in many different ways. But when it happens like this, like it is now for your mum, it is a mysterious and gentle thing to witness. Please don't be scared. She is in no pain, I promise you that. Soon, her hands and feet will be cold, bringing all remaining energy and heat to the vital organs of the body, until each one starts to shut down. Her heart will be the last, her heart will beat until she is dead. We don't know how long it will take. We can't rush it. We will just follow it and let it guide us for as long as it takes.'

It is dark now. Annie and Luke are here too, both sat upon a mound of cushions that have accumulated around the bed. She has been unconscious without movement at all on her back for a few hours. I can't look anywhere else but at her – and then suddenly, as if the air between us all moved, I am aware that death is as close as the breath at my nose. It is between us. Waiting like skin on the walls.

Sarah must have felt it enter the room too, because she has got up from her seat in the corner to come to Mum's side to feel her pulse, and now she is counting the seconds between deep and rattling breaths, which are long and at irregular intervals. Her eyes raise to Dad, Matthew, Annie, Luke and I – our faces all ravaged in stillness.

Once again, I can feel that thin veil between life and death collapsing, and I am again both inside and outside of time.

'She's almost there. Almost there. You're almost there, Tessa. It's OK, my lovely. It's OK to go. It's OK to go.'

And then, like a loose seam, so easily torn, death pulls her away. Her next breath doesn't come. There is only unfathomable, continuing silence where the sounds of her have always been.

Silence.

Rain, still pattering at the window.

Her body, cooling and silent, like a cathedral at midnight.

❖ ❖ ❖

I have lain awake all night since she was taken away by the undertaker at 1.30am, astonished blood throbbing around my heart and at my skull. Now the morning is breaking into itself at my window, the ceiling of the sky lifting into a lilac dawn. I can hear blackbirds beating air through their wings around the roof of the house. The buzzing of a bluebottle fly at the window. Then the crackling silence of the room. I am spinning on a completely new axis, unearthed, in this bedroom that I have only known in an entirely different life, one that Mum and I inhabited together – which has now ended.

I roll over to feel that I am still here and, without thinking it through, I turn on my phone to check what time it is. It instantly starts convulsing with a tsunami of incoming voice and text messages.

Oh god.

Oh no.

People know.

My brain flinches, which makes my eyes grip closed. Although I'm still lying down, I suddenly feel very dizzy, and then like I might vomit. How can it be real in other places already? Proliferating the knowledge of her death is making more 'death' of her than I can comprehend yet. I can understand it has happened here, but I'm not ready to accept that it has happened everywhere else too.

The dizziness rises into panic in my collarbones and I jump up with an urgent need to call the undertaker.

I realise I didn't remember to ask him his name. Dad must have asked his name. How could we have let a man we've never even met just take her like that? I try to retrace what happened: he arrived dressed in a black suit, white shirt and black hat. His eyes stayed focused on the floor on the landing the whole time until the nurses said she was ready to go. Then, when I said I wanted to go with her to the morgue, he said I couldn't because it was too late to have family there – so we just let him take her.

Dad said he thought I should go upstairs while they took her out and because my ears were still filled with the sound of wailing I couldn't think straight, so I just did what he said. But now I can't stop thinking about where she is at this precise moment and all the things I should have done before they took her away. I know they didn't put a coat on her, so I should have checked that the jumper we chose to dress her in was thick enough to keep her warm. I want to go and lie next to her again to check she's OK. I don't care if she's cold and silent because that is still *her* actual body and if *her* actual body *is* still here, then maybe she hasn't totally gone to death yet?

We Are Each Other

After they took her away last night, I took the pyjama top that she died in and put it under my pillow. It has deep creases around the armpits and I can smell her skin in it. It has death inside it too; I know it does because when I hold it I want to rub it inside my eyes because that is where she is now, in death. I don't want to ever be clean of death because that is the last thing I have left of her to touch. I feel so entirely with death now too that it's possible that I look like that thin quality of twilight too – translucent.

Suddenly that feeling of panic rises up into my collarbones again, so I jump up and go and hide the pyjama top in my drawer because I don't want death to take it too. It will be safer there.

I go out onto the landing outside my room and walk slow, cautious steps downstairs to the doorway of her bedroom, bracing myself for the scene that awaits: the simplicity of golden morning sunshine hitting the bed just as it did when she was inside it. But she has disappeared. The bed is made.

Her reading glasses are on the bedside table. Her clothes are laid over the armchair in the corner of the room and the room smells like her. One of her shoes is upturned as they were the last time she took them off – but now they look completely flat and without the forward impetus of life, because the person that once wore them has disappeared.

Death is making her bedroom scream at me in decibels of silence, so I leave without fully entering it. Instead, I go downstairs. I can hear the radio already on in the kitchen but I don't want to see anyone, not even Dad if he is going to make her more dead than she already is, so I take the first exit I can find and open the front door to sit on the step alone in the early morning sun. My senses are overwhelmed by the brilliant clarity of daylight and the cacophony of sound: crows cawing, the wings of blackbirds beating the air around them, swallows diving through the sky which is pulsating over fluorescent green chestnut trees – it is completely psychedelic.

Is this where you are now? Supercharging the space that is within and between *everything*?

I cross my hands around my chest so I am holding myself under my armpits with one breast in each hand to feel that I am still inside my body. My breasts in my hands feel small, soft and emptied, and then I remember the photo Finn sent me last night of Ottie in one of her pyjama sets from Mum, her bottle filled with normal milk in her hands, smiling with a milk moustache like a Cheshire cat. While I've been with Mum while she was dying, Ottie had enough separation from me to be fully weaned, so my milk has stopped.

With my hands at my empty breasts, that timeless, intergenerational cycle of being mothered and being a mother, which both require the exquisite pain and work of separation, is turning inside me in a place that is as deep as the valley between the living and the dead.

◆ ◆ ◆

When somebody dies, there is immediately so much practical stuff to do: admin, letters to reply to, the funeral to plan. While we are in this hinterland between her death and the funeral, my to-do list feels like a life raft. It means my brain is forced to think about practical things, which is a relief because it means that momentarily, I don't feel *completely* confused by her disappearance. I know she is 'dead' but secretly, I can't feel it. I am trying to piece together the facts – her shoes haven't been moved from under the armchair in her room for four days; my phone has stopped lighting up with her name on the screen with her calls. Also, because all the 'to-do's are still about her, it feels like we are still doing something for her, so she is still implicated in the now, in the day, in the present somehow. What coffin will *she* have? What flowers should we choose for *her*? What music will we play for *her*? What readings? Who will speak? The one that makes my brain clench, and I know it did for Dad too, is: will *she* be buried or cremated?

Dad said he knew *she* would want to be cremated. My response to this was instant – 'OK, but we're not burying her ashes though, are we, Dad?'

'Of course not, *she's* not going into the ground, *she's* coming home with us.'

We know that technically *she* has died but we are not ready for her to be treated like the dead yet.

Then there's her eulogy. Now that *she* is dead, we will never have anything else to add to the fabric of our relationship – the entire shape of it is complete and writing her eulogy requires me to look at it in its finite entirety. And in doing so, I already know this: I have been raised by Mum and Dad inside a big and loving

We Are Each Other

family, but the love from my mum has been the central and most important pillar upon which the rest of my life has been built. Everything I am has been made from what her love has given me. I know too that this is why I cannot just disappear into this grief – because through it all, it is my job to be building an equivalent world for Ottie. While I am washed away by a tsunami at night, I must be rebuilt for Ottie by dawn.

❖ ❖ ❖

The hearse arrives around the corner in slow, quiet, black, ritual form. Mum's shocking pink and coral peonies at the front of the house bow their heads at its arrival. I reach down and pick one stem to take with me. Dad, Matthew and I climb into the back of the hearse. It smells of new leather and sickly floral air freshener. We drive slowly down the lane, in silence, past every twist, turn and summer hedgerow that has been the backdrop to our family life, but now with the silent cracking of the earth's core happening inside and between us.

We arrive at the church. Cars are parked on verges and down the whole stretch of the lane towards its ancient wooden gateway. Cow parsley is framing the pathway through the gates to the church – billowing, exquisite white lace. We lift her coffin out of the hearse covered in peonies and Dad, Matthew and I, with the undertakers, carry her down the gravel path. The church bells chime in the sky above us like iron angels. I can't feel my legs or my face.

Jonathan is waiting with his bagpipes as we arrive at the doorway. The wailing melody of 'The Skye Boat Song' begins as we carry her into the church. It is filled to bursting with wet eyes and faces everywhere. When I am called up to speak, it is hard to read the words in front of me because as I move my eyes across the page, everything feels like it is moving, which feels like vertigo.

After the service, Dad, Matthew and I climb back into the hearse to take her to the crematorium. Dad plays 'Mahogany' by Diana Ross, which soundtracks the ten seconds it takes for her to mechanically disappear behind a lime green cotton curtain. There is a disorientating lack of ceremony to this moment that is over too quickly. We are told we will have to wait for her ashes to be delivered. We are driven home in the hearse. We cannot speak to each other and quite quickly that silence feels like a new era of distance between us.

❖ ❖ ❖

By the time we arrive back at Lower Farm after the funeral and crematorium, I know I have never felt as lonely as I do walking in the back door of the house to the sight of my whole family: Finn, Nicolette, Ottie, Annie, Luke, Eleanor, Matthew, Dad, my nieces.

As the kettle boils, I am confronted with the shock and horror that the funeral has ended, everyone is here except Mum, and there is nothing left on my 'to-do' list that she could still be even implied in. The page is now empty. The house starts to fill with more people: uncles, aunts, family friends, cousins. I can hear someone laughing at one point and I want to walk over and smack their cup of tea and plate of cake out of their hands and tell them to get the fuck out of the house. But I don't because I am suddenly distracted by Mum's sweet peas scenting the air around the kitchen windows, making my brain spasm with an instant reflex to search for her.

Finn doesn't leave my side. Nicolette moves close to me, like a loving shadow – she is always just a few feet away with Ottie on her hip, so close that I occasionally smell flutters of her Chanel No 5 and feel the soft touch of her hand at my back. At one moment, I feel so overcome with love and gratitude for Nicolette that I throw my arms around her and tell I love her. Then she puts her palm to my face and tells me she loves me too, like her own. Which makes both of our eyes fill with water, as more people start to hover next to me, trying to talk to me, commenting on Mum's eulogy, how 'strong' I had been, how big Ottie is now, asking me if I want another cup of tea. But I can't concentrate on what they are saying because I am silently planning my exit, my drive back to London to bang at her door in north London until she opens it.

Everyone else has gone.

It is quiet everywhere in the house now and we are all silent – waiting, searching for her voice, for a glimpse of her body.

In the midst of life, we are in death.

◆ ◆ ◆

We Are Each Other

Dad turns off the hob on the cooker, walks out and locks the toilet door. It is quiet until I hear muffled crying through the walls.

◆ ◆ ◆

The horror is the silence.

◆ ◆ ◆

In the three weeks following Mum's death, the natural world and everything around me was amplified in a cacophony of effervescence and aliveness: the skies never glistened as blue; I heard the air moving round the beating wings of every bird and each low-flying bumblebee, and the slow rustle of the iridescent green leaves on the trees crackled inside my ears and eyes. I do not know the scientific or psychological reason for this, but my assumption, and one I didn't question because it felt so clear to me, was that I was witnessing what I imagine in religion has been described as the ascension of the spirit. I imagined that Mum's spirit was supercharging the natural world as she returned to be *within* it. That she was now *in* the space between each molecule, each atom. In everything, everywhere.

Yet in recent days, this has changed – I have been trying so hard but I cannot locate her anywhere anymore. There is no cacophony at all. Where she once was, there is now just silence. Nothing. Just complete non-being, which is stark and plain. I am experiencing a constant, frantic internal feeling of searching for her under the beds and in cupboards at her flat, at Lower Farm, anywhere she could possibly be – and with each space I find empty, the realisation that she is just completely gone from *everything*, *everywhere* rises like hysteria into my throat.

Yesterday afternoon, I was walking round the block trying to get Ottie to sleep, while this feeling of ransacking the planet for her started again and the panic of not finding her took me to my knees. At one point I had to stop walking and crouch down with one hand at my mouth to stop Ottie from hearing a small moan from coming out of me, with the other hand at the handlebar of the buggy, still rocking her back and forward.

◆ ◆ ◆

I am woken from thin, agitated sleep by a hot spike of adrenaline that kicks me at the base of my stomach.

We Are Each Other

My eyes try to blink to open, thick and leaden with sleeping pills, my stomach clenches and I lay still, feeling the claws of grief baring and ready at my skin. I inhale through my nose, unable to prepare for what I am waking to. As cool oxygen hits at the back of my throat, grief grips deep into my stomach and my eardrums start to throb with my blood, which is loud and certain with knowing:

She is dead. She is dead. She will always be gone from me.

I sit up to try to push this murderous feeling away, but there is no way to create any distance from it. My life now, where Mum is dead, has been here all night, swinging in perpetual suspension above me, and I will be inside it now everywhere I go. I sit very still and focus, because if I focus hard enough, I will be able to find that feeling of *her* and that will stop these vicious claws from preying on me when I am sleeping. But instead, my heart starts to beat harder at my chest bone because as I search to find her face, my brain can't render her at all – there is only a black blur where her face and body as a living and animated person should be. Trying to remember her feels like the panic of searching – the frantic feeling of trying to gather up any part of her. Death has whittled her down from being a real 'person' to the precarity of 'memory'.

She is in my blood, in the space between everything that I am, yet I cannot touch her. I cannot remember her.

When does death end? When can I feel as if Mum lived, not only that she has died? Why won't my brain let me find her? Why can't I find the feelings or memories of her alive? An image of her doing something entirely mundane, like making a cup of tea, the expression on her face when choosing between having a fizzy water or a glass of wine? I told myself so many times towards the end that I would make sure I would always be able to find the feeling of her. I thought I would be able to keep her so close to me that I might sometimes feel her come through so truly that she could cast a shadow over my skin.

I thought I could pull at the threads of our memories until the sails of them would billow and we would be alive again inside a moment that was so completely ordinary it was as if death had never happened to us.

But I was wrong. She belongs to death now. How could I have been so stupid?

Death wins.

The simple horror is: I will never see her again. I will never feel the way she makes me feel again. I understand now why we have created belief systems in the form of religion which give the possibility of eternal life. Because coming into true knowing and acceptance of all death takes from us is so unbearable for the human soul to fathom that we avoid its truth at all costs. The true story of death and all it takes from us is just too painful for us to bear – so we have created other ones, where death isn't the end for the person who has died; it is just the beginning of a new life for them that we can't see or be physically part of.

Just the possibility that it *is* going on *somewhere else* allows us to feel somehow more connected to them, connected to ourselves, because the possibility of them still exists. We embed and reinforce this possibility into our language – she didn't 'die', she 'passed away'. 'Passed away', somehow not gone, just moved on to the next place, so that death is not an end stop, there is continuity, and in that continuity, there is a possibility of a time when we may be reunited. And, my god, I wish with every atom in my being that I felt this was true, that the spiritual consolation I leaned on when she was ill could soften death for me too – but the awful truth is: I don't feel she is eternally alive at all. I have never felt her to be more dead, more gone from me than she is at this moment. I cannot bear this feeling of her non-being; I want death to feel different, I want it to change. I want it to feel more magical and I am calling on the supernatural to prove me wrong. Often at night these past few weeks since she died, I have lain on my bed with my eyes pushing against the air to try to bring her through it. But there is nothing there.

My room is thick with the orange flare of London's streetlamps at night, and I push my voice gently against it. 'Mum, Mum?' Maybe if I just say it as if a response is unimportant I can trick my brain into letting her come through. My brain is not letting me find her because my brain thinks she is dead, but if I say her name in a completely ordinary way, maybe it will let me find her. 'Mum. Mum. Mum? Mum . . .' I say it loud enough so that it sounds normal and real. For this to work, I probably need to say it like I mean it – but I also need to be quiet enough so as to not wake Finn, who is fast asleep next to me. 'Mum.'

As I am saying her name – as I am searching to find and insert the living feeling of her into the unapologetically plain silence and nothingness that her death has left – I realise something else . . . I'm saying her name not only to search for *her* but to search for *me* – for who I am only in my relationship with her. I am searching for the parts of me that have died with her too. I am saying 'Mum' to feel like her daughter again. Her death has torn me at the seam of my being. 'I am broken in two,' we say when our hearts are broken, and now I understand why.

The tremendous simplicity of this knowledge has arrived with no nuance.

I roll over in bed and I disturb Finn, and he turns in his sleep and pulls me into his warm chest and stomach to hold me like land emerging from the flood. How can I tell him I have woken, drowning, in the chaos and terror of a tsunami? It is impossible to – so I just lie and let him hold me: driftwood.

Then I hear the shuffling sounds of Ottie tugging at the side of her cot in her room next door. I go into her and she is standing at the side of the cot rubbing her eyes, not crying but on her feet with sleepy arms and cub-sized hands reaching up to me. I lift her out and we climb into the bed next to hers. Shuffling across the cool underside of the duvet, we curl up in the middle, her knees up to her tummy, my arms holding her from her shoulders to the curve of her bottom – our foreheads and noses touching. I start to hum 'The Skye Boat Song', which cloaks us like a hymn. Her bright black, feathery eyes are blinking slowly, like butterfly wings.

We curl into each other with this loss, this love, destroying and recreating me all at once. It is as deep as the earth's crust, twisting the land to rise into new mountain ranges.

As I look into Ottie's face, and feel her growing body in my arms, I remember again that I am still here and with so much living of my own yet to do. Death has smashed my sense of time and motion, but Ottie is a river and when I focus on her, even in this moment, I can feel my sights rise to a horizon again. Ottie is my forward thrust of time in a world that otherwise, since Mum's death, feels like it contains very little movement. The part of me that existed only in my relationship with

We Are Each Other

Mum has died, but when I am with Ottie, though I am partly dead, I am also burning with life.

And so we lie, with that same orange flare from the city leaning into the room, but with Ottie in my arms, I can feel the roots of my greatest sorrow and my greatest joy meet and entwine with surprising intimacy. Cool, quiet tears drip over the arch of my nose onto hers. I wipe them from her as if they are poison.

Ottie's tiny voice rises from her tiny chest. 'Mumma', 'Mumma', 'Mummy' she says into the dark, like I do, but when she says it, she sounds instead like she is describing a universe. 'Mumma', 'Mummy' – it is a word that bolts me to the world again.

With Ottie in my arms, I realise the length of each breath is increasing, finding some space at the base of my stomach again. So I just lie, listening to her tiny voice saying 'Mumma' into the room until we both fall back to sleep.

◆ ◆ ◆

I startle awake to the crack of knocking at the front door. I reach for the bedside clock and see we have slept into the middle of the morning. The house is unusually quiet and there's a note from Finn next to the bed – 'I had to leave early but didn't want to wake you both. Call me when you're up, I love you.'

I stumble out of bed, pulling Ottie up over my shoulder, her body and face still heavy and warm with sleep at my neck, and I walk downstairs, one hand on the banister to steady me, and open the door to find the postman. He tries to hand me a cluster of letters, but there are too many to hold so he places them in bands inside the door. I close the door – my thoughts are congested with sleeping pills, my stomach is twisting into a grey knot. I stare down at the hall floor, which is covered with envelopes.

There is no angle of normality which grief can't make into an object of sorrow. Even the symmetry of these rectangular envelopes is cruel in their presumption of the ordinary, the profound and the ordinary always side by side. I pull Ottie in closer, so her knees are pushing under my ribcage, and I stare at the bundles with a sudden heat of anger. I don't want them. Hundreds of well-intentioned cards and letters confirming the unchangeable fact of her death.

Each one will contain a message from a person who

is powerless to change it and usually unequipped to deliver the small mercy of true consolation: 'how awful for you', 'how heartbreaking', 'how shocking', 'how unbearable', 'how cruel', 'how tragic for your family'. Every single one of those words makes it worse, with their bland platitudes that don't say anything about this loss and how it has killed so many parts of my existence.

Why is it that death and grief, the only universal and inevitable experiences of life, are so difficult for us to talk about? Why hasn't an articulate, vivid and exact language for it emerged? Without it, every day since Mum died, I have read well-meaning letters or looked into the faces of visitors who avert their awkward gaze and confirm the loneliness I feel with well-intentioned platitudes, devoid of any sense of true knowing: 'I can't even begin to imagine what you are going through.' Every time someone says this to me it is like being kicked in the gut. How lucky to be so, so far away from death that you simply cannot even imagine it, because I *can* imagine it, because every waking moment of each day, I am being forced by death to live within the astonishing and terrible clarity of what it has done.

Jess Mills

The blandness of words like 'terrible loss' and 'condolences' are repeatedly offered to me as tokens of well-meaning sympathy, but these words run like vast, cold waters between me and the rest of the world, confirming what I already know: I am on the archipelago, all bridges are down. I do not want to seem churlish or ungrateful for genuine sympathy, but the honest truth is I've never felt as lonely as I do among these hundreds of letters from well-meaning people. They arrive as an avalanche at my door and just confirm that the obliterative details of the experience of loss seem to have no place in the imaginations of those whose lives are whole. They are kept in the shadows. Though I do at least understand why – because it would be *terrifying* to love, to *live*, if we truly accepted what death can touch.

Yet, later, I *will* sit and brave each letter, because there may be just one sentence that leans in, knowing there is no way or need to fix me – and in doing so, it may pull me closer to the world again.

◆ ◆ ◆

I have noticed something new emerging in recent days, that if I choose not to stare into the vortex of everything we have lost and instead choose to focus, I mean really focus like a mantra, on everything we have had together — there is a sudden and extraordinary feeling of the cellular knowledge of it all inside of me, glowing like a golden orb in my chest. And for those moments, I feel like the luckiest person on earth to have known her love at all. So I am trying to do this more.

After all, impermanence is the only thing that is certain. How foolish of me to have lived my life without paying closer attention to that.

❖ ❖ ❖

Mum's death has done violent things to my ordinary suppositions. Now, it is as if the whole world I live within has broken. I have been cut off from the source of the longest love I have known. The central pillar of my family, the person who is my deepest sense of home, has disappeared. Since I grew inside her body, Mum's voice has always been one which has spoken and, I realise now, I never questioned that it was destined to always speak. Her death is laying the absurdity of all my presumptions pathetically bare. It feels unsafe to love now in a world where I know in that matter of my flesh that nothing is protected from death.

I think this must explain a recurring dream I have started having. It began the week after Mum's funeral and I had it again last night. The narrative is of infidelity – I find a girl naked in mine and Finn's bed at home. Last night, it was someone I was at university with, looking as she looked as she did when we were 22, armoured with her lithe and intoxicating beauty. Within moments of the dream starting, I realised Finn was also in our bed with her, and he started to move towards her in ways I only know as being mine – until his arms were wrapped around her from behind, his hands holding onto her stomach and breasts, and she was arching for him to be inside her. He looked right at me and all I could see in his eyes was the grip of him wanting this person, who is not me.

Each time I've woken from this dream in the last few weeks, the residue of the feeling of betrayal, confusion, heartache and rage I feel as I am watching them together clings to me throughout the day. But it is not a mystery to me what this dream is about: it is only now that it has vanished from my life that I realise that the unconditionality of my mum's love has been the anchor that has allowed me to feel safe in loving and receiving love from the rest of the world – maybe because unconsciously I have always assumed that if absolutely everything else was taken away from me, she would still be there. Now she is gone, nothing feels secure.

Looking again at my life now, without her in it, is like searching through the remains of a sunken ship which have risen, now floating on the surface of the sea. I can see in the wreck that there are indeed many parts of my life which her death didn't take, but there are so many unexpected parts of my world which sank to the depths of death with her, never to be touched, felt or seen in the same way again. And I realise that these lost parts of my life, the parts that sank into death with her too, are now the localities in which this grief plays out in its rawest and most elemental form. One of them is my sense of 'home'.

Since that moment the undertaker took her away at 1.30am on May 13th, there has been a cruel and, I now suspect, irrevocable death of the magic of Lower Farm – where every morning, the light is still hitting Mum's bed like it did when she was asleep inside it.

Mum is not a ghost in the house – she has disappeared from it completely. The *life* we had there together is the ghost, and it has made a ghost of everything in it: the ticking of the grandfather clock, the clunking sound of the letter box, the smell of lavender and rose in her drawers of untouched folded clothes, the rabbit teddy sat upright in Ottie's cot, the perfectly ordinary sight of her navy blue waterproof coat hanging in the hallway, the susurration of the silver birch tree leaves, the surrounding hills calling out to us to walk within them again. It was 'Mum' who was our home. So now when we are in the house and the landscape which has been our home for decades, we all feel homesick. We cannot be let into the world we had with her, without her.

I thought about what death would do to Mum, and to our family, constantly after her diagnosis. But I didn't think because it didn't occur to me about what it would do to the way our family operates. How her disappearance would change the way we function, the way we *are* together.

Families are both physical and psychological entities, and in ours, she was the connective tissue of both. Without her now, the construct of our family unit feels like it is in a landslide, collapsing; we are unable to hold the form of our family together as we were. She was the person who pulled us into each other. Even as she was dying, she was still so alive to us that we were seeking in her the strength she created in each of us, wanting her, to be the truest witness of us.

Such is the death of a person who lived and loved as prolifically as my mum, that all those who were bound into her through family and friendship know the bitter truth of her death by the pure and certain shock it has sent into their lives. But I can already feel how the world outside our immediate family, that was briefly so affected by her death, is already beginning to resume. So individually obliterated by it are Dad, Matthew, my elder siblings and I, that, as a result, right now, we are not opening up to each other and supporting each other through it – in many ways, we have never felt so far away from each other. I never question their unconditional love for me or mine for them, and I do not feel that anyone has done or is doing anything wrong, yet it is nonetheless a stark and disorientating new dynamic to come to terms with –

observing how the physics of loss plays out, how it has created a scattering of us that is beyond our control.

I have stood in plain sight of Dad many times these past few weeks, my eyes and throat bulging with grief, only to have to swallow it down, because he is so deep in a fortress of his own sorrow that he cannot register mine. Dad and Mum had a world together, one which I will never truly know, because it was his and hers alone – a life of 42 years of marriage, so now even the map of his own body leads him in irreconcilable searches for her.

I know, for all of us, that the empty seat at the table is never more stark than when we are together. This is why being together at the moment is too painful – because '*we*', our family, is the locality where her absence plays out most acutely.

Ottie isn't happy at Lower Farm either anymore. We went to visit Dad at the weekend and she saw Mum's picture on the landing as we were coming downstairs for breakfast. Then we walked slowly past Mum's bedroom and I instinctively closed the door to her room. Instead of asking for her like she normally does, Ottie cried. She was fraught all weekend, hurting with a feeling she is too little to understand or even have words for. She kept throwing plates of food that Dad had made her on the floor and point-blank refused to get into her car seat when we were trying to venture out for a walk. Then she had the worst and longest meltdown she's ever had. I was so defeated by it that we didn't go out in the end. Instead, we stayed at the house and I cried into the crease of my elbow in the toilet while Finn paced around the kitchen with Ottie in his arms till she eventually calmed down.

Throughout the weekend, she kept saying 'Ganny?' and I could feel she was angry with me because it is a question I cannot answer. I worry that I don't know where my sadness ends and where hers begins – I don't want her to become my sorrow. But this weekend, I am sure Ottie was aching with loss which is her own. Her crying when she had another meltdown in the garden before we left was the sound of grief, visceral and vivid.

It is certainly true that infants and toddlers are not developmentally mature enough to fully understand the concept of death. In fact, many children do not fully understand the concept of the inevitability and permanence of death until adolescence, but it has been proven that even babies grieve. Surely, if you are old enough to love then you are old enough to grieve?

I realise now that I look back over Mum's life as if it was partly mine. The future without her in it is a death of a future that was only possible by us both being in it. This is multiplied by the future she will not be in for Ottie too, so this loss feels as deep as the generations, because it is. And of all the losses for the future – the intergenerational loss of her not being in Ottie's life now is the hardest to make peace with.

❖ ❖ ❖

I'm starting to think that, in a life with an existential loss at the centre, making radical changes makes most sense. Without thinking it through, in a brittle moment on the phone to Dad today, I said that maybe we should sell Lower Farm. He didn't disagree. He just didn't say anything in response. But for a moment, as he was walking down the lane outside Lower Farm alone, I heard a shift in the tone of his voice, that suggested, for a moment, he had been able to imagine an entirely new and different future.

— *Summer 2018* —

A fragile lunar light pours through breaking, soaring skies. Condensation sparkles in prisms on the window. My eyes are thick with sleep. I focus into the landscape beyond the old stone window frame: navy blue and purple contours of towering, prehistoric mountains are rising into the violet dawn sky.

The map of the West of Scotland looks like the left wing of a monarch butterfly. Plockton is positioned at the widest point of the left wingspan, on the shores of Loch Carron, facing inland, east, away from the prevailing Atlantic winds. This little fishing hamlet is cupped by the land that surrounds it, creating a microclimate which is so ambrosial in summer that cordyline palms and sugar-pink frangipane line the shores of the ice-cold sea loch. Plockton is so far north that the night sky in summer never deepens beyond the cobalt blue of a lunar eclipse. Just like the Celtic Saints had described, the light, the landscape here, has that 'thin' quality. The veil between earth and heaven here is porous.

I have come here, to this place that we never made it to together, with my heart bloodied and ripened to the start of decomposition. But within the decay of loss, within the mysterious clarity and absolute 'thinness' of this place, I can observe how the shoots of new life are starting to grow.

Yesterday, Dad and Matthew met Annie and I from the train in Glasgow and we drove four hours to this waterside cottage, through landscapes of untamed mountain basins that hold vast sea lochs in the palms of their hands; through panoramic vistas of mauves and verdant greens, where mediaeval coal-black castles perch on metallic shorelines like raven crows. The skies here billow like moving sheets of ivory and lilac silk, continuously reanimating the landscape in wild and moving colour. Here, I feel as small as a pebble on the water's edge.

We drove until the coastline opened its wings at its most westerly point into the Kyle of Lochalsh and, as it did, Dad's driving started to slow and our eyes raised to meet the Isle of Skye, who stood before us like a heroine – her slate black, deep green wilderness connected to the mainland by the arms of her bridge, spread wide. As we rolled to a stop, layby gravel spat at the wheels of the car and we all instinctively wound the windows down so that the car filled with herbaceous air, perfumed with licks of salt from the sea loch that separates Skye from the mainland. Dad turned off the engine and we stepped out into a breeze that felt charged with whispers and knowing; the acid-yellow gorse rustled, an occasional lone car passed, white stone crofts peaked like flags on the hill and a single eagle soared overhead, its magnificent wings spread over mountainsides of pines that cast jagged, pitch-black silhouettes against the sky.

We all stood separately as the breeze blew and stared into the expanse. The space between us was so alive with her absence that we stood in silence. I was sure for a moment that this was because Matthew, Annie and Dad were listening close like I was, trying to hear her. After a few moments, Dad turned from the view and walked back towards the car, gravel crunching underfoot. Then his seat belt clunked as our cue to reassemble our positions in the car and drive the short, winding distance over the plateau that descends into Plockton along the water's edge, up to the door of our B&B, which sits on the one- track lane overlooking Loch Carran.

We dropped our bags and then walked side by side to the local pub. I realised, looking at each of their faces, that for months we've been completely out of focus to each other because we have all been completely engulfed by our individual grief.

We walked through the tinkling bell of the old wooden doorway, under dark wood-beamed ceilings, to the bar which is as wide and low as a single arm span. Elton John's 'Tiny Dancer' was playing on the radio to a bar not yet filled with its early evening regulars. We stood pondering the draft ales, wines and baskets of crisps. We each got a glass of the white wine, a local favourite Mum often recalled drinking too much of

We Are Each Other

after a long walk with her girlfriends, and walked out to find a bench on the jetty to sit down, facing the water with the majesty of the Highlands towering around us.

Weathered white bunting hung like page-blank prayer flags over the wall to the water's edge; lobster cages were piled up. A small white fishing boat disturbed the mirrored surface of the loch to create a train of ripples in the perfect reflection of the mountains. We watched as the boat dropped its anchor to moor beyond the swimming buoys. The skin of swollen bellied trout was dancing prisms at the water's surface, which quivered every few minutes, alive from the surface to the prehistoric depths of its bed. The air was rich and knotted with the scents of pine and frangipane, having been heated throughout the day and now risen to fill the air. With every flux and shift of light, I could feel my heart starting to flicker like a lightbulb in a storm.

We sat as the lowering sun danced in beams across us, turning our wine glasses to liquid gold in our hands, the cool air feathering our faces. We avoided talking about her. Instead, our eyes shuffled over the menu. We remarked on the reasonable price of the scallops.

Then we refilled our glasses with her favourite wine, drank two bottles empty. I watched Dad watch nothing, as if the world behind his eyes had collapsed outwards and was now lying empty in front of him. Her absence covers everything.

We ate the scallops but didn't stay long. After walking the hundred metres back to the B&B, before going to our rooms, we turned and gave each other a kiss and planned to meet at breakfast in the morning. Once in my tiny snug of a bedroom I lay down, and for the first time in weeks, I felt sleepy. I found myself following it, slipping fully clothed into a deep and gentle sleep that held me until now, at dawn.

The morning meets me with its purple and blue mountains, rising with the promise of a bright, still day. As the sun lifts into the sky, I walk alone, following the map of Mum's stories, to the end of the village and the jetty she told me about so many times. How it was positioned in the most beautiful view she knew, how she chugged through these exact waters to collect scallops for her supper.

I arrive and stand at the far end of the jetty, looking

down into the deep, crystal-clear, ice-blue water. She would always call me when she came to this spot – planning when we'd eventually come here together, wanting me to be in the moment of its beauty with her too. I feel my love for her, and her love for me, which is as deep as the sky, suddenly ignite in me like tiny white lights in the centre of each of my cells, until I feel what I can only describe as being as illuminated as a star fallen out of the sky and standing on the water's edge in broad daylight. Without thinking, I start to undress. How could anything be hidden under a sky so wide and open? I step to the edge of the jetty and, before I can think, I dive.

The skin-splitting cold hits like needles into my skin and skull – it is so sublime it is startling, bringing me into absolute presence with all that is here, with all that is still so, so alive. I climb out up the steel ladder, breathless, and lie with a speeding blue and white sky above me, my membranes breathing wet and naked to the air, like crustaceans on the seabed at low tide, in cool and simple intimacy with the air, the water, in this expanse where living and dying are so intimately known by nature's great cycle of life.

Her death, and my living, suddenly hold a different tension. All at once, I am in focus again.

Death takes so much. It takes worlds and universes, but there are some things it can never take.

It cannot take love.

◆ ◆ ◆

As the weeks approaching the midsummer weekend that Finn and I had originally held for our wedding party started to quicken, the dilemma of whether we can hold any kind of celebration during mourning evolve from being a question to a command: Live.

Nothing has created a greater clarity about the privilege of being alive, and about the finite opportunity to live, than Mum's death. So we are doing the wedding party this weekend at Shimpling as planned – not in spite of her death, but because of it.

Shimpling is the only place for this party. Here, I have noticed that I feel distance and separation from the black holes of loss that are devouring other places in my life, like they are at Lower Farm. I am observing here how it feels like grief is only inside me and not inside everything else. There is something about grief which is a yearning within the body as inescapable as a feeling of hunger – but one that you cannot feed. All retch and no vomit. At Shimpling, I am noticing how that hungry yearning eases. It is the only place where I feel my heart and my body rests – aided certainly by the way Nicolette positions me by the fire with blankets and cups of Earl Grey tea, the sight of her taking Ottie off, her tiny hand in hers, to pick flowers in the garden together.

Sitting by the crackling fire, I can feel how a new shape of life, which is entirely separate and distinct from the rest of my family, is becoming more visible to me. A shadowy, fragile new chrysalis. Of course, this is not a place where I will ever experience my own mother's love, but I know I feel these things because *the* mother's love flows through every part of being here – because of Nicolette. 'Welcome home, darling', she said to me, her palm at my face, when we arrived here a few days ago.

❖ ❖ ❖

Finn and I turn to face each other under the towering 200-year-old sequoia tree, the congregation of our friends and extended family strewn around us upon the bright green stripes of the newly mown lawn. They are so uncharacteristically quiet that I can hear the rustling sound of the peroxide-blonde barley fields that backdrop the garden moving like whispered secrets. The garden is surrounded by the peaks of white tents, ancient oak trees adorned with huge disco balls, a shimmering silver cocktail bar, a stage and towering sound system, which has a pair of inflatable legs akimbo with lurid red stilettos perched on the end, each leg as tall as a double-decker bus. Overhead, the swooping black crosses of swallows dart across the fading blue sky, which is splashed with liquid gold and silver clouds.

As the sun dips, it beams into the garden sharply from the west, and the garden becomes its own stage, filled with every living person in the world who we love, their faces floodlit with tangerine light. When it strikes Finn and I, the silver sequins covering the entirety of my dress shoot refracting lights across the front of the 500-year-old house. This moment feels like a beam of biblical sunshine, broken through black clouds.

We Are Each Other

As our celebrant reads our vows, I am unable to stop myself searching the faces of the crowd for Mum. But as I do, I recall as a firm instruction to myself the beautiful and important advice given to me by a friend recently, whose mother is also dead. She said: 'Even while you are grieving, you must try to remember the living.' I repeat this to myself and I squeeze Finn's hands tighter in mine. I look back out to the crowd and my eyes catch Nicolette's. Ottie is curled into her arms asleep at her neck, surrounded by my best friends, by Matthew, Annie, Luke, Eleanor and my dad, now all handing out glasses of champagne to the sea of faces on the lawn.

It is a mysterious and merciful experience, observing how agony and ecstasy entwine with such ease, in knowing intimacy – supercharging and electrifying each other. Grief is the subatomic, imperceptible stripe in the rainbow that you can't always see, but it is always there, making the other colours burn more vividly.

Just to be alive. Just to be alive. Just to be alive.

— *Autumn 2018* —

It is autumn again, the time of year in London when at night, the sky sinks into the belly of the city, and in the early morning, the streets smell sweet with the cool decay of rotting leaves that fill doorsteps and pavements on every road. Among the thinning tones of the trees lining the streets in London this year, I realise that I am now able to see a whole new dimension to human existence around me. It's a bit like being able to see ghosts, but instead of seeing the dead, I see people who walk around with the experience of death inside them, like I do. I am drawn to these people, people like me, who are passing through the wasteland of their lives, entirely confused as a very ordinary red bus drives through it and the doors open and people get on and off and the ticket machine beeps and then it drives on. People who are picking their children up from school or having a seemingly ordinary conversation with someone at work while their soul is screaming at the wall of death to open and let their loved one come back through to them.

I was certain that the woman in front of me in the queue for the checkout at the supermarket this morning had death smudged in her eyes like I did for weeks after Mum died. She was younger than me, maybe in her late twenties, dark brown roots and a ponytail of bleach-blonde hair. A naturally striking and beautiful face, with that skin of grief that looks like twilight around her eyes. The Spice Girls' 'Wannabe' was playing on the supermarket radio, the irregular and persistent bleep of tins of tomatoes, baby milk and nappies being checked through by the checkout assistants over it. At first, I recognised something familiar in the quick and panicked reflex of lifting her baby boy out of his buggy as he started to grizzle, the silent edge of desperation in her eyes while pleading with her toddler, now lying on the floor, to hold onto her hand and not run off – her expression was holding more than just the frazzle of having young children. Then I saw her boyfriend's keen and attentive eyes on her as she raised her wrist to her eyes to wipe her tears so her toddler wouldn't notice. I recognised the look on her boyfriend's face too, the distance he kept from her, which held a degree of caution. I could see how he was not sure how to touch her, even when tears were now spilling out of her eyes, because she was on fire with that particular kind of grief that was creating a ring around her, between them, and everything.

Living with Mum's death inside me this summer has done something to my sense of boundaries. Previously, I would have kept a more usual, or appropriate, distance. But instead, without thinking, I found myself stepping towards her and asking quietly, 'Are you OK?' And this unlocked a profound and knowing look of relief and recognition between us, so that within moments, water started pouring silently out of our eyes, as ordinarily as rain down a window pane. Each of our children were still hanging off our legs.

We spoke for five minutes. She told me that her younger brother had recently died by suicide. I told her about Mum. We hugged each other with an immediate intimacy, in a way I have never done with a stranger before. In the silent agony of her tears, in the way her head involuntarily lowered heavy onto my shoulder, in the subtle slump of her whole weight onto me for a fleeting moment as she resisted the urge to collapse – I knew that her body, like mine, contains the visceral knowledge of how death so simply moves over our screams as we are separated from someone we love for eternity.

Within seconds, we were pulled apart by both of our children creating havoc in the checkout aisle. We forgot to ask each other's names. This kind of mutual, naked recognition of how loss reveals that 'we are each other' at a soul level has reminded me that I am still here, still. It has confirmed that my experience of loss isn't a black hole – it is one lone star in a universe of others.

What has happened to me, to my family, has been life-defining for us, but it is far from extraordinary. Quite the opposite. It is entirely ordinary. Grief and loss is the everyday apocalypse that is happening in every corner of life, but it happens on our insides, so no one can see it.

Every day since Mum died, I have observed how difficult it is for people to engage with my grief. So I too have got very skilled at being able to mask it. But occasionally, the primal wailing feeling of missing her roars through me so ferociously that it tears my skin, and then there is this terrible sense of being unable to stop my insides spilling out in public when I start to cry. But I've realised too that at least if I cry, the pain is visible and then people can respond to it. I have noticed I feel most fraught with Finn when I am being mauled by missing her in plain sight, but he cannot see it because it looks like I am just making dinner – and it's also important and vital that I am. I can no longer wait for the daily, exquisite agony of missing to cease in order to start living again. I need to re-enter the land of living. The work of living again must commence. While I would do anything to be held close by her soft arms and stomach and love that is so huge and certain between us, I have soft arms and a soft stomach now too – and while her work as a mother has now ended, mine has only just begun.

◆ ◆ ◆

There are times in life when our universe implodes and it feels like all the beauty and light gets sucked into a wailing black hole. But what I have learned is that sometimes this particular darkness is not static – it can be a space of tremendous movement. And in that wild and unpredictable place, under the cover of that darkness, huge transformations can take place. And when you emerge from it, you realise that the darkness wasn't terminal, it was incubating the painful emergence of a new life. Because often, the experience of a new life emerging is an experience of the unbearable, isn't it? I think, looking at Ottie's shoulders and all her kicking limbs that emerged out of my body 18 months ago, now the shape of a glorious toddler, almost completely filling her buggy.

For 18 months, I have been walking along both sides of new life and death, and it has required my body to hold a tremendous and often unbearable experience of pain at a soul level. But it has also taught me to stay patient and alert to the little miracles nestled in the ordinary. Of all of them, I think the most extraordinary and simple of all is this: that even after the most unbearable of times, more gentle times can, and do, come.

◆ ◆ ◆

Today, five months after Mum's funeral service, we are having a memorial service for her at Southwark Cathedral in central London. We have invited everyone she knew and loved to come and celebrate her life and to mourn her death. In this majestic cathedral with its ancient stone walls and serenity, with over 2,000 people around us, I feel I am now able to look at the whole shape of her life – to feel for the first time that she lived, and not only that she died.

Just as I was about to say goodbye to Matthew on the phone last night after talking through last arrangements for today, he said, 'I know you are still navigating the huge hole Mum has left in your life, but I just wanted you to know, I don't think I've ever seen you more whole.'

Perhaps, in experiencing the death of someone at

the epicentre of our world, rendering us partly dead too, we can access a new capacity to burn even more deeply with life, making us somehow twice alive. If we listen and look then nature tells us every year: new life and death spin on the same wheel.

Today, as I prepare to step up in front of the cathedral, I do not feel the torture of searching for her anymore; the knowledge and fact of her death is inside me now. So I am able to experience how profoundly important this very human ritual of celebrating life and mourning death is. It is older than recorded time or history, and it does now what I suspect it always has done for those who remain – it holds the utterly surreal reality of life without your loved one still, in its palm, inviting you to be brave, to look at it.

Being alive means that sometimes awful, obliterative things will happen, and when they do, the body will have no choice but to accommodate unbearable amounts of pain and sadness at a soul level. But if we can keep going, keep going, keep on going – to see through another minute, another hour, another morning, another day, another night – there might come a moment when you are aware that while that pain has created an entirely new shape of you, it is not *all* that you are. You may then be rewarded with an entirely unexpected and life-changing gift – that of being truly awakened into this life and to all that this fleeting moment of being alive still offers.

Grief has gotten inside all of my cells and awakened them, awakened me truly to life – so I feel now as if I am beginning to inhabit this new shape that I am, and my own ultimately fleeting and finite moment of existence.

As I stand up to walk to the lectern with Matthew and Dad on either side of me, the cool autumnal air of the cathedral between our shoulders and a sea of eyes and faces in front of us, Dad steps towards me and offers me his arm, and Matthew reaches down and squeezes my hand, and then winks at me out of his left eye in the exact way Mum used to. We have all been changed so much by her death but ultimately, we are still being changed by her love.

If I were to dig down into the deepest pit of this grief, to discover what is in its molecules, I suspect I would find that grief is not made up of the molecules of death at all but is made from the molecules of love.

As I step towards the lectern to say my opening words, I think, maybe death doesn't win after all: love does.

◆ ◆ ◆

I wake this morning, the morning after the memorial service, and, before I open my eyes, I feel tears filling my eye sockets with that raw and primal feeling of yearning for Mum that feels like my blood is wailing. With Ottie and Finn already out at the park, I lie alone doing the only thing I can think of whenever this happens. I say her name – 'Mum, Mum, Mum' – and I keep saying it under my breath until the word becomes breath again.

The astonishingly simple and unfixable thing that her death makes me feel is: I miss her. I miss her. I miss her.

Instead of staying there too long I do what I try to do now when my blood starts to wail. I get up quickly, call Finn and get myself out the door, into the forward thrust of the outside world.

Standing here in the park with them, I can feel in my chest how my heart is still blood raw, but I also know now that I am surviving.

We Are Each Other

The cold air of autumn is at my ears and at the back of my throat, the rusty metal chains of the swings are grinding back and forth, and Ottie's intermittent shrieks of joy are lighting up her luminous black eyes as I tickle her knees when the swing brings her towards me. The trees surrounding the playground are towering above me like a cathedral. Their leaves are once again hanging by their threads: temporary jewels of ruby red, amber and emerald green.

And then, still within the cathedral of trees, something comes to me that is not like a thought but more like trying to listen, closely, for something completely intangible – a familiar song in my blood which I can't quite name until I lift Ottie out of the swing towards my chest and my breasts feel hard and sore as I pull her into me. I put her in her buggy and tell Finn I'll meet him back at the house, then walk alone to the chemist on the high street and buy a pregnancy test.

Once I get home, Ottie is sleeping, so I go straight up to the bathroom, rip open the foil packet with my teeth and pee on the stick. Within seconds, there it is: two vivid blue lines.

Jess Mills

Once again, I have two heartbeats.

I stay perched on the cold edge of the bath, with those same chalky white floorboards under my feet that I gave birth to Ottie upon, full-throated with this news, and with a sudden and breathtaking sensation that renders Mum more vividly to me than I have felt since she died. Once again, I can feel that the arms and hands of separation are reaching, outstretched between us. But now they are outstretched from our cells – in the cycle of life that continues, that not even death can break.

— *Epilogue* —

Legacy is the energetic afterglow of living. Sometimes, a person's legacy is so powerful that they will continue to change the world even though they have died. This has been the extraordinary thing I have witnessed since Mum's death, and it has changed my life in unexpected ways.

After she died, I became the CEO and founder of the Tessa Jowell Foundation, which I began in order to be the custodian of her legacy and, most immediately, to ensure that her dying wish to transform brain cancer treatment and care across the UK was delivered.

With the support of the Tessa Jowell Foundation and a growing list of some 95 other partners across the

UK, the Tessa Jowell Brain Cancer Mission (which was formed immediately after her campaign speech in the House of Lords) has grown into a national effort for change. We now work with every adult and paediatric NHS brain cancer hospital in the UK through our Tessa Jowell Centre of Excellence initiative, aiming to transform research, treatment and care. It is our ambition that by doing this work, we will be able to change outcomes for brain cancer patients for this and future generations.

The Tessa Jowell Foundation raises money to fund this work, which has already been commended by the NHS as 'unprecedented' and 'exemplary'. This is of course a profound way to honour Mum's legacy but, ultimately, as she would want, it is for the thousands of people and families like ours, for whom there is now a reason for hope.

However, I have come to learn that her greatest legacy of all, where her lifeforce burns brighter and brighter the more time passes, is not in relation to the things she achieved but the person she was. Distilled, it is the way she loved the world around her and how she was loved by the world in return. It is the single

We Are Each Other

greatest privilege of my life to have been her daughter and to have been held in the epicentre of this love until I was an adult myself.

Nine months after the chronological end of this book, my second pregnancy grew beyond my body and I gave birth to another daughter. We named her 'Hero'. Four weeks after Hero was born, Matthew became a father for the first time to his daughter, Skye Tessa Mills, who has eyes the colour of pale blue sapphires.

Ottie, Hero, Skye, and now Skye's little sister May, aren't babies anymore. They are little girls who astonish me when they sing 'The Skye Boat Song' to each other, or by the particularly familiar way Ottie and Hero call me 'Mumma'. Mum is in these songs we sing, in the daily lavender bubble baths me and my daughters have, in the flowers we put by our beds in vases, in the landscapes we all walk in. Ultimately, *she is in the way we are able to love and be loved by each other.*

I think that these very quiet expressions, which ripple and resonate down the generations, which are the continuum of how and by whom we have been most loved, are the greatest legacy anyone could wish for, bringing us as close to immortality as we can get.

The summer Hero and Skye were born, my dad sold Lower Farm and moved to a flat near Matthew in London. It had become a mausoleum of the past and, while the absence of a family home has had a profound impact on how and where our family is able to come together now, it was necessary in order to free us from the torment of being there without her. It also made us take a radical and important step forward into the new world without her.

That summer, the whole house was packed up and, for the first time in 43 years, some of Mum and Dad's possessions were divided. Mum's clothes, shoes, books, bath oils, crockery and photographs were boxed up. Dad took some, some were put into storage and the other boxes me and Matthew divided between us and then stored at home, for as long as we needed to be able to face their contents.

It took me three and a half years to be able to open them. It was winter again, almost Christmas. By now, the furnace of new grief had mercifully cooled, but the festive season was shining a spotlight on Mum's absence and forcing me to look at it, whether I wanted to or not. In particular, the build-up to Christmas was making claws bare in my stomach at the fact that Mum had never known Hero and that Hero had never experienced the feeling of her love.

By this point, Ottie would often dream about 'Granny Tessie'. She would talk about her, refer to how she 'loves' her in the present tense.

Before we packed up to drive to Shimpling for Christmas, I felt a sudden and strong impetus to start on Mum's unopened boxes and decided to begin with the boxes labelled 'Photos'. Inside them were mainly photo frames, pictures of friends, of the family. In one box, there was just photographs of me and Ottie together, many I didn't realise she'd had printed. But in between these photos of me and Ottie, with those claws now feeling hot in my stomach, I came across a little object I'd never seen before: a small, blue-grey wooden frame with a little wooden painted boat in the middle, sailing under a black-painted sky filled with white-painted stars.

I looked closer at this little picture, it being the only thing in the box I didn't recognise. On the side of the little black and red boat in the middle of the picture was written this single word: 'Hero'. On the back of the frame the words: 'Hero sailing by night'. The name of the granddaughter she never knew, who came to me as the greatest offering of life, the day after her memorial service.

Of course, grief is infinite because love is infinite too. Magic, even.

— *Acknowledgements* —

Thanks, firstly, to Ottie and Hero – miraculous daughters who are the ultimate purpose of everything – and to Finn, who, over the five years I was writing this book, did absolutely everything conceivable to make the writing of it possible, other than actually writing it.

To Dad and Matthew, for your love and utterly uncomplicated and open approach to my capturing this time – of which you both have your own equivalent stories of the love and loss of Mum to tell.

To Nicolette, for being our homestead, for doing everything you can to make me feel the presence of 'the mother's' love still in my life, and for loving Ottie and Hero with the presence and adoration of two grandmothers.

Jess Mills

To Luke, and to my sisters Eleanor and Annie, for the love and care they took in reading the rawest early material and giving me the critique, encouragement, and confidence to continue.

To my manager, Marc Shienman, for making the pivotal introduction to Jonathan Lloyd, Lucy Morris and Rachel Goldblatt at Curtis Brown. Jonathan, Lucy and Rachel – my agents and editors – your meticulous brilliance, your imaginative and deep editorial work on me and on this book were continual torchlights in the long and patient work of finishing it and it being published. And to my publisher Carole Tonkinson who received the manuscript with such passion, commitment and care to preserve it as you received it, and Saira Nabi, Flora Willis and Arabella Watkiss at Leap/Bonnier for publishing it with such love and ambition.

To my girlfriends – too many to name, but you know who you are – the other greatest loves of my life, who don't all feature so much in the pages of this book, but who held me throughout and beyond.

Lastly, to Mum. Everything I am, everything in these pages is made from the love you gave me. I love you forever.